Brewing Sustainability in the Coffee and Tea Industries

T0328092

This book focuses on the often intertwined industries of coffee and tea, using accounts of single producer communities to highlight the transformation from plantation-style colonial agriculture towards systems that now claim to produce social and environmental benefits from the farm to the cup.

Focusing on the dynamics of farmers' experiences producing coffee and tea ethically and sustainably at origin, the book shows how these values are transmitted and reinforced throughout the value chain. Exploring tandem case studies of fair trade cooperatives in Guatemala and Sri Lanka, it provides an insight into the creation of more sustainable value chains from producer to consumer in the global marketplace, incorporating the perspectives of coffee exporters, importers, roasters, and café owners. This book is focused on the prospects of the specialty movement in food as a catalyst for forging more authentic, just, and sustainable supply chains that consider both people and the environment.

This book will be of great interest to students and scholars of food and agriculture, sustainable food systems and supply chains, the fair trade movement, sustainable development, and social entrepreneurship and social innovation.

Alissa Bilfield is a faculty member in the Food Systems, Nutrition, and Health Program in Nutritional Sciences in the School of Public Health at the University of Washington in Seattle, USA. Her interdisciplinary background includes work and research in the government, nonprofit, and academic sectors that has spanned the United States, and 14 different countries, ranging from Guatemala to Sri Lanka. She is also a social entrepreneur herself, having co-founded a food literacy and cooking education nonprofit called The Cookbook Project.

Other Books in the Earthscan Food and Agriculture Series

Deep Agroecology and the Homeric Epics
Global Cultural Reforms for a Natural-Systems Agriculture
John W. Head

Fighting for Farming Justice
Diversity, Food Access and the USDA
Terri R. Jett

Political Ecology of Industrial Crops
Edited by Abubakari Ahmed and Alexandros Gasparatos

The Sociology of Food and Agriculture
3rd Edition
Michael Carolan

The Politics of Food Provisioning in Colombia
Agrarian Movements and Negotiations with the State
Felipe Roa-Clavijo

The Governance of Agriculture in Post-Brexit UK
Edited by Irene Antonopoulos, Matt Bell, Aleksandra Čavoški and Ludivine Petetin

The United Nations' Declaration on Peasants' Rights
Edited by Mariagrazia Alabrese, Adriana Bessa, Margherita Brunori, Pier Filippo Giuggioli

The Agricultural Dilemma
How Not to Feed the World
Glenn Davis Stone

For more information about this series, please visit: https://www.routledge.com/Earthscan-Food-and-Agriculture/book-series/ECEFA

Brewing Sustainability in the Coffee and Tea Industries

From Producer to Consumer

Alissa Bilfield

Routledge
Taylor & Francis Group

LONDON AND NEW YORK

First published 2022
by Routledge
4 Park Square, Milton Park, Abingdon, Oxon OX14 4RN

and by Routledge
605 Third Avenue, New York, NY 10158

Routledge is an imprint of the Taylor & Francis Group, an informa business

British Library Cataloguing-in-Publication Data
A catalogue record for this book is available from the British Library

Library of Congress Cataloging-in-Publication Data
A catalog record has been requested for this book

ISBN: 978-1-032-13357-7 (hbk)
ISBN: 978-1-032-13358-4 (pbk)
ISBN: 978-1-003-22885-1 (ebk)

DOI: 10.4324/9781003228851

Typeset in Times New Roman
by MPS Limited, Dehradun

This book is dedicated to smallholder farmers around the world. May your success and dedication to sustainability improve your lives and your communities, while serving as an example of ingenuity and potential for coffee, tea, and food systems sustainability at large.

Contents

Figures

Tables

Introduction: A Brewing Novice

This book is about sustainability in the coffee and tea industries. It is about how these beloved beverages have transformed the way that producers produce and consumers consume. Coffee and tea both rely on a complex natural process involving plants that once grew wild, but now thanks to the ingenuity of humans, have been domesticated and widely cultivated around the world. Even with the insidious rise of soda in the 20th century, tea is still the second most popular beverage in the world, just below water. Coffee, though less sipped than tea by volume, is second only to crude oil in terms of its value. Neither of these products is particularly essential for human nutrition. Yet, the majority of us could not fathom a single day without one or the other, or perhaps both. Some scholars have posited that this is due to our innate drive toward consciousness-altering substances, a way for us to get through the monotony of the days, to motivate us to do our work with more inspiration. But mostly, these drinks make us feel better. Indeed, the caffeine content in both beverages has been proven to induce a sense of elevated wakefulness, clarity of mind, and creativity of spirit. Others would argue that it is the communal, ritualistic, and cultural value of these products which inevitably bring us together around the ancient hearth or the modern-day tea and coffee shops of the world. These beverages have been intertwined in human history for thousands of years.

When I was younger, I was unaware of what it meant to drink an authentic cup of coffee or tea, let alone what went into getting it from the farm to the cup. My mother devoutly drank instant Folgers, mixed with a heaping spoonful of powdered creamer and half of a bright pink packet of sweetener. My father was always seen with a Starbucks coffee cup in his hand, so I had no real reference point for 'brewing' coffee. It was no wonder then, that I was first drawn to drinking tea. It seemed easy enough to steep a bag of tea in hot water. I learned from

DOI: 10.4324/9781003228851-1

my grandfather the divine nature of the sugar cube, and I came to see these saccharine delights as a treat to be taken with tea. Occasionally, if I was feeling sophisticated, I would add lemon or honey. Little did I realize I was dabbling along the edges of a vast tradition of brewed beverages that stretched back millennia. My eventual obsession with specialty coffee would follow, almost a decade and a half later.

It was not until I was a junior in college living in Nashville, Tennessee, that I became aware of tea in its traditional loose-leaf form. One day when I was window shopping in Hillsboro village, I stumbled into Davis Cookware and Supply, a small family-run shop for gourmands which sat on a prominent street corner adjacent to the Vanderbilt University campus. The shop was run by two enigmatic brothers who were as devoted to keeping alive the art of southern hospitality as they were to maintaining the chaos of their somehow charmingly disheveled shop. Each brother was passionately obsessed with the fine art of caffeination. One through the brewing of coffee, and the other through the steeping of tea. Upon opening the old creaky wooden door, you would be hit with the enticingly sweet and aromatic scent of nutty roasted coffee beans, which would mellow as you approached the counter. On your way in, it was all you could do to avoid knocking over any number of expensive kitchen gadgets that had been lovingly squeezed into every corner of the space. I curiously approached the counter, unsure of what exactly to anticipate next. One of the brothers, the tea brother, emerged from the piles of boxes that lie below the counter. He had rosy cheeks and thinning long hair. He glowed with a kind of unexpected well-being. Our eyes locked, and I could tell I was going to be in for quite an experience.

After innocently enquiring for some Earl Grey tea, the only type of tea I really knew about at the time, I found myself being pulled willingly into the expansive world of specialty tea leaves. The tea man, as I came to call him, began enthusiastically recommending tea types. Genmaicha, a Milky Oolong, perhaps a smoky Lapsang Souchong? Each tea had its own unique shade ranging from bright green to dark velvety black. The shapes and sizes of the leaves varied from straight to gnarled and curly. At the time, it was astounding to me that all these seemingly different teas came from one plant, *Camellia sinensis*. In his earnest desire to share and spread his passion for specialty teas, I left Davis Cookware that day with at least half a dozen smaller packets filled with samples from the tea man. He also delivered on my original request for Earl Grey. Luckily the shop also sold the necessary steeping devices, and I parted with a few extra dollars and purchased a proper strainer for loose-leaf brewing. Little did I imagine that over a decade and a half later my fascination with tea would take me halfway across the world. That I would be tromping through the heavily armed golden triangle amidst the green tea-filled mountainsides of Myanmar or convening with tea farmers in the hill country of Sri Lanka.

Although tea has always been my primary fascination, I was perpetually intrigued by coffee as a child. Perhaps it was because it seemed to be a coveted beverage for adults, who could not pass a single day without it. When I was much younger, too young to drink coffee, I would beg my parents for a sip of the black nectar and then I would pretend that the bitter brew was delicious. But mostly I dabbled in coffee ice cream or chocolate-covered espresso beans. When I was in college I imbibed in the auto-drip variety, mostly for the curious and exciting effect it had on both my creativity and my digestive tract. It wasn't until I began studying coffee as a PhD student later in life that I became initiated into the cult of specialty coffee. It was not intentional that I ended up studying coffee as a PhD candidate. Rather, I had intended to focus my PhD work around the topic of the double burden of malnutrition, using Guatemala as a case study. While many scholars of nutrition know that Guatemala has one of the highest rates of child mortality, due in a large part to malnutrition, it has only become a recent phenomenon that obesity has become a growing crisis as well. This double burden of malnutrition is a complex, multi-layered problem with structural roots bound up in the social and economic determinants of health. I received a small amount of funding to conduct formative research and caught a flight to Guatemala City.

While I was in Guatemala on this initial research trip, I met with a number of inspiring and dedicated individuals all working to address the complex nutrition problems plaguing the country in their own ways. They were all attempting to move the needle on childhood malnutrition through a variety of approaches, ranging from hybrid fortified corn and bean seeds, to cooking classes or through traditional nutrition-based epidemiological studies. But, what none of these interventions really addressed directly and sustainably was the unavoidable reality of poverty, which was at the root of childhood malnutrition and food insecurity. Without the ability to earn a reliable income, to live in a safe and stable home, to have access to food, basic nutrition would be an impossibility. But how to thread the needle on such a complex problem with entrenched structural roots? Guatemala is still a predominantly agricultural country, and at the center of many agricultural communities in Guatemala are cooperatives, often comprised of smaller community development groups. What really caught my attention was not necessarily the work of international development organizations or clinical academicians, but the work of the cooperative organizations in Guatemala, run by farmers themselves. It seemed, at least from what I could observe, that they were getting at the root of the problem by addressing poverty through livelihoods in solidarity with community. More importantly, these organizations served as centers of power for otherwise disparately populated rural communities with few resources. And in Guatemala, the vast majority of cooperatives are not organized around the growing export market for broccoli, or green beans, but around cash crops such as coffee – the country's third-largest export.

This is how, as part of my doctoral research, I ended up passed time sitting atop burlap sacks of coffee beans in the Huehuetenango region of Guatemala while eating tamales with women coffee farmers as we discussed their lives. At the coffee cooperative's office, they would prepare a simple medium roast. No milk, no sugar. Just the delicious essence of the coffee grown from the surrounding hillsides. Before my experience in Guatemala, I had enjoyed any number of well-made espresso drinks, and I had begun to brew my own dark roast. Like any good American, I believed that dark roast meant stronger flavor and maximum caffeine content. I had not yet experienced the depth of flavor and variety of tastes that coffee could offer, especially the finer medium and light roasts that preserved more layers of flavor and actually served up a higher dose of caffeine. Until my time in Guatemala, I was also unaware of the distinct differences between *Robusta* and *Arabica*, or the importance of water temperature and water purity to the brewing process. Also eluding me was the importance of where the beans are grown, how they are grown, how they are roasted, ground, brewed, and then enjoyed. Now, you can find me in the early morning grinding my own coffee beans. When I am off traveling around the world, I always pack the essentials: a bag of well-roasted beans, my hand grinder, and my stainless-steel coffee filter.

While I began this journey steeping, brewing, and sipping the most formative parts along the way have been tracing tea and coffee from the farmer to the cup. Along this journey, I have gained insights about the evolution of these two conjoined industries from the farmers' perspective. The big questions this book seeks to address are focused on the major shifts that have occurred in the last few decades in the coffee and tea industries. These shifts have led to the transformation of coffee and tea supply chains, and have resulted in the emergence of more ethical and sustainable approaches in the global marketplace. How can these beloved beverages be produced more ethically and sustainably? What are the challenges that farmers and their collaborators face in these efforts? Perhaps most importantly, how can we learn from the progress made in the coffee and tea industries to integrate these systems of sustainability as models for other industries? The goal of this book is to better understand how these two intertwined crops are becoming more sustainable through a variety of organizational, economic, and socio-cultural forces.

From 2015 to 2020, I had the opportunity to explore the dynamics of the movement toward sustainability in the coffee and tea industries through two case studies. Both endeavors were formal academic studies that went through rigorous IRB approval in the United States and the countries where the research was conducted. The coffee study was focused in Guatemala. I traveled to coffee expos in Puebla, Mexico, and Seattle, Washington. I also traveled across the variable landscape of specialty and craft coffee purveyors and retailers in Europe, the Americas, and Asia. Perhaps most importantly, the coffee study focused on exploring the perspectives and experiences of specialty coffee farmers who are members of an indigenous Mayan fair trade organic coffee cooperative that is part of a larger federation. Through this research, I interviewed 30 farmers, 20 supply chain stakeholders, and conducted significant direct observation and document analysis. The main goal was to understand farmer and supply chain perspectives on how the coffee industry has transformed over time and the implications of current sustainability practices on the future of their livelihoods. In particular, the coffee research focused on gender equity and broader issues of social sustainability.

The tea study was focused in Sri Lanka and took me to the world tea expo in Las Vegas, Nevada, as well as across various tea-drinking communities in India, Nepal, Myanmar, and China. In Sri Lanka, I learned about the tea industry through the perspectives of tea cooperative members, from the largest cooperative organization in Southeast Asia. Similar to the coffee research, 30 farmers were interviewed alongside 20 supply chain stakeholders, with significant direct observation. Mirroring the coffee study, the main goal was to understand farmer and supply chain perspectives on how the tea industry has transformed over time and the implications of current sustainability practices on the future of their livelihoods. In particular, the tea research focused on issues of environmental sustainability.

All of this research relied heavily upon grounded theory, which is based on forming insights related to data and observations, as opposed to a predetermined framework or theory. In the case of the coffee research, several art-based participatory research methods were also utilized. In the Guatemala study, life landscape drawings were used in combination with interviews to allow farmers to visually depict their farm homesteads. This research tool also allowed study participants to feel more comfortable sharing during the interview process. The photovoice technique was also used in this study, which invites research participants to share their perspectives through photography. As opposed to quantitative research, which seeks to understand the phenomenon through generalizable statistics, this qualitative research had the goal of understanding the commonalities and variabilities in the farmer experience and the breadth of their perspectives as members of fair trade cooperative organizations. They not only shared their experiences as cooperative members but also shared their perspectives on sustainable livelihoods and organic farming. The results are stories, insights, and opinions as opposed to statistically generalizable means, medians, and modes.

The core of this book shares the farmer's perspective from two separate research studies on these topics as they relate to sustainability as it is more broadly conceived. The book has been structured into three parts and triangulates the perspectives of supply chain stakeholders and secondary research from the coffee and tea industries.

The first part traces the origins of coffee and tea through colonial history with a focus on the major transformations that have occurred up until the most recent trends in these intertwined industries. This part also provides a definition and framing of sustainability around the economy, society, and the environment. In addition, this section describes the pre-eminent sustainable business certifications related to agriculture. Finally, this section provides more specific context of the history of coffee and Guatemala and the history of tea in Sri Lanka as a backdrop for the case studies. The second part of the book is focused entirely on the case studies. Each chapter focused on a different aspect of sustainability: economic, social, and environmental.

The third part evaluates supply chain stakeholder perspectives and discusses broader insights from the cases for application across other agricultural industries and beyond. Overall, the book highlights how farmers are integrating sustainability practices at the individual level through their production approaches, and at the organizational level through the relationships they forge along the supply chain. For the first time, this book brings together research from the two seemingly unrelated case studies in a dynamic way. The content narrates how the forces of colonization, development, globalized markets, and the rise of sustainable business have created new approaches to sustainability and models that have scalable value to create impact.

Acknowledgments

This book would not have been possible without the collective effort, time, and energy of so many different people involved in the coffee and tea industries, and the world of academia. Part of this research was conducted during my tenure as a doctoral candidate, and so first and foremost, I would like to acknowledge my doctoral dissertation committee, Dr. Diego Rose, Dr. David Seal, Dr. Ted Fischer, and Dr. Erin Peacock, for their support and guidance throughout the research process. Each of their unique perspectives and worldviews has helped me to unearth and shed light on distinct aspects of this research, from the fieldwork to the final conclusions.

While in Guatemala, it was truly a blessing to work with the co-operative members in Huehuetenango and to hear their stories and perspectives. I am also grateful to have been welcomed into the facilities, workshops, and meetings of the cooperative and the coffee federation. I am fortunate for the assistance of many friends and colleagues living in Guatemala: Daniel Buchbinder from Alterna for introducing me to the coffee federation. Nidia Gomez and Juan Francisco Gonzalez Menchu from the coffee federation for their collaboration, steadfast determination, and inspiring enthusiasm. Valentina Santacruz, for her assistance in arranging my Guatemalan research permit, and Josh Wood for arranging the majority of transportation logistics. To my Spanish translator Ingrid Morán, many thanks for sharing your gift of language, and perhaps most importantly to the head of the cooperative at the time, Luis Bravo, and my six research assistants for their open-mindedness, trustworthiness, patience, and love of green mangos. I learned so much from you, and you were both intrepid and dedicated.

While in Sri Lanka, I had the good fortune of working with a dynamic network of cooperative members who were willing to share their experiences. I appreciate being welcomed into the facilities, homes, and offices of the cooperative and the tea federation. I am fortunate for the assistance of Padmasiri Wanigasundera, Wijerathne Dutuwewa, Jeewaka Bandara, Sharath Ranaweera, Madusha Ranaweera, and many others. To my Sinhalese translator and an amazing scholar and practitioner in her own right, Kumudu Ariyawanse. Perhaps most importantly, many thanks to my four research assistants for their open-mindedness, trustworthiness, patience, and love of rice and curry. Your support has helped shed light on farmers' perspectives on sustainability.

This research was supported by generous funding from the John Snow International Doctoral Travel Grant, The Tulane Taylor Center for Social Innovation and Entrepreneurship, The Penny Jessop Travel

Fund, the Mary Amelia Center for Excellence in Maternal and Child Health Doctoral Training Fellowship, and the McGuire Center for Entrepreneurship. Without such support, this research would not have been possible.

Finally, to my personal support structure. First to my family and friends for their truly unbelievable faith in my dedication to the daily writing ritual. From an early, age, my parents supported my writing, from the limericks to the term papers. My siblings and friends were always there to share a cup of coffee or tea when I needed it most, especially my sister Shana, my brother Brandon, the members of Endless Galfest, the Vandy Ladies, and most recently Mya Sherman. To all of the places that I called home throughout the research and writing of this book. First and foremost, to the city of New Orleans, for the necessary celebrations amidst the grind of a doctoral program. To the city of Tucson for the desert trails that offered time for reflection, and to the city of Seattle for steeping me in coffee culture while I perched in my chair, writing. I would be remiss for not mentioning my dogs for their happy company at strange hours of the morning and night, one of whom, Hoogli, served as a constant muse throughout the process. Last but certainly not least, to my partners in life during this time. One was there for the beginning, and the other for the end. Adam: you hiked alongside me in the Ixil triangle and searched out the best street food and train snacks across Guatemala and Sri Lanka. Matthew: you were pulled unwittingly into months of writing and editing and early morning coffee brewing and tea steeping. Your edits and insights have been indispensable.

Perhaps most importantly, before we begin, a dedication to smallholder farmers around the world. May your success and dedication to sustainability improve your lives and your communities, while serving as an example of ingenuity and potential for coffee, tea, and food systems sustainability at large.

Part I
The History

1 Transforming the Daily Cup

Introduction

The botanical origins of coffee and tea are separated by thousands of miles. Yet, because of history and colonization, these two beverages have become intertwined. First, we must understand the relationship between coffee, tea, and systems that comprise these two industries. This next chapter compares and contrasts the origins and connected rise of coffee and tea from their precolonial domestication to their current global reach. A great deal has been written about this subject by historians and botanists, both equally intrigued by these two transcendent beverages. Although not the central focus of this book, a briefing on these origins provides the requisite context for understanding current and future trends in sustainability in regards to these industries. Perhaps most importantly, it also provides critical background for understanding the current perspectives and experiences of farmers, traders, and consumers.

At the material level, the most obvious similarities of tea and coffee are that they are both beverages of plant origin that are steeped in water. The inspiring and addictive effects of these beverages on the human body cannot be underestimated as motivation for their sustained spread throughout the world. Both of these beverages feature the stimulating compound caffeine, alongside several other key metabolites. This is where the plants diverge in effect. Some claim that coffee produces more of a jolt with a crash, while tea produces more of an energizing and steady effect that plateaus. Either way, both contain caffeine, an addictive drug that creates a sense of elevated wakefulness within its user. A dearth of scientific research has been conducted over the last century on this topic. Those who are interested in the most recent compendium can consult *Teas, Cocoa and Coffee: Plant Secondary Metabolites and Health* by Drs. Crosier, Ashihara, and Toma's-Barberan.[1] In their

DOI: 10.4324/9781003228851-3

eloquent scientific tome, they provide an extensive and detailed summation of the mythological origins of each beloved plant stimulant. Perhaps most importantly, they describe the compelling physical impact of caffeine and associated plant alkaloids on human health with attention to bioavailability, absorption, and metabolism.

Caffeine may be a major part of why coffee and tea have become so popular, but how did these beverages become so widely available? This is a curiosity that food historians have been contemplating for decades, with a new volume being written about the subject and released regularly. While writing and research stretches back centuries, a few recent scholars have summarized their predecessors' work for our benefit. Current writing on the topic blends history, anthropology, sociology, political science, economics, and business to elucidate how coffee and tea have transformed the world.[2,3,4,5,6] The precolonial histories of these beverages, which are known in the zeitgeist through a variety of popular mythologies, give some insight into what drove the globalization of coffee and tea.

Origins and Domestication

Tea

Unlike coffee, tea has a longer domesticated history by a few thousand years. The origins of tea are steeped in Buddhist mythology. One of the most well-known legends dates to the Tang dynasty in China. Bodhidharma, the founder of Chan Buddhism, accidentally fell asleep after meditating in front of a wall for nine years. When he awoke, he cut off his eyelids in frustration at his weakness. The eyelids, tealeaf shaped, fell to the ground and took root, growing into tea bushes. Various other myths and stories recount tea's entrance into human society.[7] However, tea historians now believe that the original wild tea trees that predate domestication likely spanned a larger geographic region. This region spanned from India to the modern-day Chinese border in Yunnan through to Myanmar, Laos, and Vietnam.[8] That said, domestication of the plant, though still disputed, was likely in China according to the botanical record.[9] The original tea economy in these areas was based on the labor and care of small family farms, unlike the large-scale tea plantation model that churns out the volume of tea we enjoy today. Historically, tea in China and its other countries of origin had been predominantly managed by families. More labor-intensive aspects of production were then coordinated at the village level.[10]

Tea, as many would assume, comes from a leaf identified by modern science as *Camellia sinensis*, with leaves that grow on a bush or tree. What fewer people realize is how that leaf comes to resemble the dark colored, sometimes powdered substance that is often found inside of a teabag. Tea grows best in warm humid climates, from sea level to the higher altitude hill country. The terroir of the land heavily influences the quality of the tea. Depending on the region, the most precious tea leaves are harvested at the first flush, which is the first picking of the top-most subtle, precious leaves. Second flush and so on continue down the line in terms of flavor and desirability. Usually, there are at least three harvests throughout the year although in some cases, as is the reality in countries such as Sri Lanka and Kenya, tea is harvested year-round.[11] While manicured and terraced tea gardens are a mesmerizing sight to behold, the origins of this now highly domesticated crop are from the wild and gnarled tea trees of South-Central Asia.

Coffee

Coffee, as fewer are aware, comes from cherries that are picked from a tree-like bush. The coffee cherries become ripe once or twice a year, are harvested, sometimes fermented, usually pulped, and then the remaining beans are dried and processed. Each bean comes from a single cherry, and the vast majority of coffee cherries are still picked by hand. Worldwide, 80% of these cherries are produced by small-holder farmers, supporting an estimated 25 million families in the developing world.[12]

The botanical history of coffee has been traced to the highland of Ethiopia, Southeastern Sudan, and Northern Kenya, at some point making its way to Yemen.[13] One of the main mythologized origin stories of coffee is from 850 AD in Abyssinia. This myth centers around a goatherd named Kaldi who noticed that some of his goats had returned to the herd with great vigor, and came to find that they had been imbibing red coffee berries.[14] The goatherd took note, and this is how humans discovered the invigorating powers of the coffee plant. Extending beyond the goat myth, legend has it that a monastic heard of the effects that the beans had on goats. Desperately trying to keep his fellow monks awake during religious ceremonies, he introduced coffee to the monastery gardens. Thus, the trees became common fixtures of monastery gardens across the Arab world, harkening its spread.[15] In Northern Africa, during the height of the Ottoman Empire, it was coffee that fueled the creativity, genius, and culture of the time. During this epoch, the popularity of coffee spread throughout the region where it became established as a key beverage from Cairo to Damascus and then to Istanbul. This resulted in the introduction of the coffee house as a meeting place where news, ideas, and politics were exchanged.[16]

Colonial Domestication

Through no coincidence, while tea was being planted by colonizers in the 1800s, coffee was being planted in tandem. While both coffee and tea were regionally prized beverages long before the colonial period, as European powers began circling the globe, they soon became two of the central commodities that fueled colonial empires. Coffee was first brought over to Europe from the Ottoman Empire. Here, colonizers stumbled upon a vast culture of coffee drinking that originated somewhere between modern-day Yemen and Ethiopia. As European colonizers came into contact with coffee across Africa and the Middle East, it soon became a prized beverage outside the Ottoman Empire.

One of the first colonial powers to usurp coffee as a crop was the Dutch. They brought coffee seeds from the Mocha region in Yemen to Indonesia, where the Dutch East India Company first started growing coffee as a colonial crop in Java during the 1690s.[17] From this point onward, coffee began to spread to other colonial outposts beyond Asia to the Caribbean and Central and South America. The modern coffee belt now spans the equator, and five of the top ten largest global producers today are in Latin America, including Guatemala.

The colonization of tea developed in tandem with the colonization of coffee. In some instances where coffee had failed to flourish more widely, it was supplanted with tea. This was the case in Sri Lanka, where a plague of coffee fungus damaged much of the coffee-growing landscape and created an opening for tea. The British East India Company had become intertwined in the Chinese tea trade in the 1800s, and in their quest to control the production of this popular commodity, they established the plantation-style model for tea production. During this period, the British developed tea plantations throughout the British empire in Asia, and then about a century later introduced tea to Kenya.[18] Thus, the global proliferation of tea can be seen as a byproduct of the empire-driven British, whose tea plantations spanned from India to Myanmar through Sri Lanka and eventually to East Africa.

In the context of colonialization, which initiated the widespread cultivation of coffee and tea around the equator, land was stolen and local populations were enslaved and indentured. During this period, the structural inequities of colonization directed the form of the early era of the global tea and coffee trade. Coffee and tea were reliant on many human hands for the harvest. As a result, the profitability of these early industries was heavily dependent on the exploitation and enslavement of indigenous and marginalized communities. These workers, they lived on-site in extremely impoverished conditions, as many still do today, their lives governed by the quantity of leaves or cherries plucked. The plantation model, while immensely profitable, only served to create a system of deeply entrenched inequity that is only now beginning to be acknowledged, addressed, and altered.[19]

The Seeds of Transformation

Many of the structural inequities of colonial attitudes, trading practices, and infrastructure remain in both the coffee and tea industries. However, a variety of forces are restructuring how these beverages are produced, traded, and consumed. The seeds of these changes, which began in the colonial era, hinted at the moral imperative that now undergirds the modern coffee and tea industries. Even during this period, there was dismay voiced at the model that was created in the coffee and tea industries. One of the most famous examples was the fictional book called *Max Havelaar*, written by Multatali about a Dutch coffee broker who campaigned against corruption and inequality in the colonial coffee trade in Indonesia.[20] It is not surprising that more than a century later the first Fairtrade-certified coffee company, Max Havelaar, was created and launched in 1989. The Dutch company takes its namesake from this symbolic colonial administrator who struggled to end the exploitation of the Indonesian peasantry in the coffee industry. Max Havelaar Coffee is emblematic of the wider shift that has taken place over the last few centuries from colonial conquest to fairer modes of trade.

The incubation of the fair trade movement is one of the early markers of this incremental shift in business practices away from the colonial model. While originally focused on the coffee industry, the modern fair trade system has spread to tea and other commodities so as to provide a safety net for coffee farmers by offering a fair price, as its name suggests. In addition, the system originally sought to promote environmentally sustainable growing practices, human rights (from gender equity to ending child labor), and it incentivized the creation and support of farmer-led agricultural cooperative organizations. In fact, it still does today. Fairtrade has grown from a social movement of patchwork grassroots organizations and non-profits in the early 20th century, to a market-based industry that serves more than 1.6 million farmers and workers with global sales that have surpassed 8.95 billion dollars.[21] As an aside to avoid future confusion, the general term for the concept of fair trade is uncapitalized, whereas named organizations are capitalized, such as Fairtrade International and Fairtrade USA.

The fair trade movement's success has been in the support of small-holder farmers and their cooperatives. While the history of the co-operative is much longer, the rise of modern cooperative agricultural organizations across the global south during the 1960s and 1970s has provided an institutional infrastructure to support small-holder farmers at each stage of the production process. The fair trade model has changed and evolved. Originally the program was limited to certifying small-holder farmer organizations in an effort to create a niche market. The system was broadly envisioned as a development mechanism to address entrenched rural poverty amongst agricultural communities by supporting economic, social, and environmental justice for cooperative organizations, small-holder farmers, and their families.

In the tea industry, this shift to cooperative organization has only just recently begun to happen. Although coffee cooperatives were gaining recognition as early as the 1970s, in tea this economic re-organization can be traced to the rise and subsequent demand for fair trade a few decades later. Coffee was the initial focus of the fair trade movement, paving the way for a plethora of other cash crops. In both coffee and tea, a byproduct of these trends has been an increased focus on supply chain transparency, especially as it relates to social, economic, and environmental issues at origin. Here, small-holder pro-ducers are managing the most labor-intensive and critical parts of growing and processing of these crops.

The penchant for ethical and sustainable goods continues to spread globally. It is one of the driving forces behind the evolution of not just the coffee and tea industries, but the good food movement, and the rise in the consumer preferences that value sustainability.[22] As commu-nication and transparency have increased, collective consumer awareness of the impacts of industries such as coffee and tea on workers and the environment has also grown exponentially. As a re-sult, more and more consumers want not only higher-quality coffee and tea, but also a connection to the producers. No longer satisfied to drink cheap commodity coffee and tea, or even country-based blends, a new wave of consumers seeks out "single origin" and "micro lot" beverages. These products advertise the exact origin of beans or tea leaves beyond the country level to regionally designated areas, even down to the actual plot of land and its farmer.[23] Historians and scholars, particularly in the coffee and tea worlds, have categorized the evolution of consumer preferences by waves, similar to the feminist movement.[24] The three major waves include the first wave of colonial commodity production, the second wave of regional and specialty production, and the third wave of craft coffee production.

In *The Craft and Science of Coffee*, published in 2016, Jonathan Morris recounts these waves in detail with attention paid to the variation in approaches. Some scholars have already begun categorizing a fourth wave, while others have observed five waves. Overall, the waves serve as a model for understanding significant shifts in the coffee and tea industries toward more sustainable practices across the supply chain.

The first wave stems directly from the colonial period of the 1800s up to the mid-20th century. This wave was focused on commodity production, volume, and value. Some scholars now separate this wave that spans nearly six centuries into two phases: the "pioneering" phase and the "industrial" phase. The pioneering phase accounts for the colonial spread and growth of coffee agriculture and consumption, while the industrial phase describes the mass commodification of coffee. The first wave, moving from the pioneering phase into the industrial phase is characterized by cheapness, consistency, and convenience. Marketing and communication around coffee during this period of the early to mid-20th century was marked by messaging around pricing and ease of preparation. First-wave coffee can be identified on supermarket shelves in large tins or containers, often featuring instant counterparts.

The second wave arose in the mid to late 20th century with companies such as Starbucks and Peets. These companies had started to value the quality of the coffee and the regional origins. Dubbed "postmodern" coffee, this wave is characterized by initially smaller roasters who set themselves up in opposition to the corporate giants of the first industrial wave of coffee production and consumption. These brands were the first of their kind to sell coffee through its origin story, connected to people and place. They were also the first brands to embrace fair trade and popularize the importance of these values within the coffee industry. Starbucks began as a roaster and wholesaler, and after taking inspiration from the coffee culture of Europe, began to evolve into the now behemoth "third space" for coffee that it is today with a global footprint of 32,938 retail locations.

As observed by the anthropologist William Roseberry, the second wave demonstrated a combination of "new coffees, more choices, more diversity, less concentration, and new capitalism."[25] In the late 20th century, the second-wave movement proliferated in the United States with the Specialty Coffee Association of America documenting a growth in specialty coffee outlets from 585 in 1989 to 29,308 in 2000.[26] These outlets distinguished themselves through authenticity and hand-crafted

Italian-style espresso-based beverages. Perhaps most notably, the second-wave movement was a departure from the first wave not only in terms of values but in terms of price-point. The value proposition was authenticity and quality, all the while demanding a higher cost per cup for the experience and connection. However, underneath the higher cost were the higher premiums being paid for better coffee beans, from more ethical sources. The second wave was not happening in a vacuum. Just like the first wave, it was influenced by sociocultural and economic trends happening at an international level.

The third wave is marked by the turn of the 21st century. This wave represents a movement in coffee that integrated the evolving values and concerns of the parallel food movements that catalyzed the creation of fair trade and other certifications. In a way, this movement represents a shift away from the scaled growth of second-wave coffee companies and the commodity exchange of the first wave to some of the original motivations of the "pioneers" of the second wave. The third wave has been a reaction to the industrialization and homogenization of second-wave coffee. This movement has proliferated globally, in part as a result of its highly mobile and digitally connected transnational community of supporters. Central to this movement is the concept of value-co-creation, where consumers adopt a more active role in the production and consumption process, said to be "prosumers" as Morris observes. Throughout this evolving industry, values around justice, sustainability, and forging authentic and transparent business relationships are communicated, and in theory integrated. While there is some consensus around the narrative and goals of the third wave, a spectrum of interpretation exists around who actually benefits from the values of this wave.

The third wave in specialty tea, just as in coffee, strives to empower consumers to change the way they drink tea. While much more has been written about this trend in coffee, the global tea industry has also witnessed a similar shift. As specialty coffee evolved from the first wave up to the third wave, so too did tea in the context of the modern cafe, restaurant, and retail environment. While regionally in tea-drinking cultures the value of tea terroir and the ritual of tea drinking has been constant, in the vast majority of countries where tea has been exported this has only recently been embraced. The first wave of tea mirrors that of coffee, where commodity tea was mass produced in bags from the "dust and fannings" of the tea process. This began to change during Tea's second wave in the 1970s and 1980s, where brands such as Tazo, The Republic of Tea, and later Teavana adopted premium positioning. Some began to offer whole leaf teas, and the packaging and pricing all reflected many of the same shared values as second wave tea. The third wave in specialty tea came next, and just as in coffee, this wave strives to empower people to change the way they conceptualize tea. Specialty tea is always whole leaf, and values the origin terroir, unique tasting notes, and functional and energetic benefits of the brew. Drawing from similar consumer bases, who are willing to pay a premium for not only a higher quality product, but one with a story and a connection to the production process and the people on the other side of the supply chain.[27] While fair trade initially ignited within the coffee industry, as the tea industry has evolved fair trade has become embedded into the specialty movement.

What do all of these shifts in the specialty coffee and tea industries portend for the sustainability of these industries? There are supporters along the spectrum: from wholesale optimists who see steady progress as practical, to critics who do not see the waves as change but rather as approaches that still replicate neo-colonial patterns of power and benefit. On one end of the spectrum, are the critics like anthropologist Dr. Edward Fischer. Dr. Fischer was a mentor of mine from my time as an undergraduate and graduate student. He has spent decades in Guatemala working alongside farming communities and even launched a social enterprise to combat childhood malnutrition. At the same time, in his published works from 2014 onward he grows increasingly critical about the benefits that the third-wave coffee movement claims to bestow. His most recent commentary suggests that "while coffee farmers receive marginal benefits, the economic value high up the supply chain continues to reproduce perpetuates classic dependency patterns of global capital accumulation."[28] Fischer is not alone in his concerns. Others, such as sociologist Daniel Jaffee who composed the acclaimed book *Brewing Justice,* and his peer Sarah Lyons who has written extensively on fair trade, are critical of the system. They claim that relatively few benefits of the third-wave movement have trickled down to producers working at the material level, still often under colonial conditions.[29] The critics of specialty tea, among them Mythri Jegasan and Devarati Sen who in their extensive research point to the vastly unequal economics of tea that still exists even with the integration of systems such as fair trade.[30,31] While cooperatives are becoming more common in the tea industry, unlike coffee, the majority of tea is still produced using the plantation model. In this modern version of the colonial plantation, seasonal workers are paid to pluck leaves paid based on the quantity they collect.

On the other end of the spectrum, mostly from the emerging disciplines of social entrepreneurship and scholars of social innovation within the business and management worlds, there is optimism about the value produced by these shifting industries. Certainly not seismic but significant. These supporters point to the relatively notable decolonization of these industries and the democratization of the global marketplace through direct-to-consumer access on social media and sales via the Internet.[32] Various scholars even argue we have now entered another wave, either fourth or fifth depending on your orientation, where valuing the producers is at the center of good coffee and tea. Those seeking to reform the system even further have shifted to embrace the concept of "direct trade," or "beyond fair trade." This is an effort to create even shorter supply chains, higher income for farmers, and more transparency of transactions in the global marketplace.[33]

Ultimately, these intertwined trends all prioritize quality and terroir over sheer quantity. They in effect elevate the highly prized Arabica coffee produced by small holders and the first flush of tea produced from a 400-year-old tea garden. While some argue that this movement only impacts a small percentage of the industry, oriented around specialty coffee and tea markets, from a functional perspective it offers a model for creating more widespread change. The next chapter delves into the details of how sustainability has been framed in the coffee and tea industries. It will also provide an overview of the major certifications that have been employed to create more sustainable systems across the value chain, while also measuring progress.

Notes

1 Alan Crosier, Hiroshi Ashihara, and Francisco Tomas-Barberan, *Teas, Cocoa and Coffee: Plant Secondary Metabolites and Health* (Wiley, 2011).
2 Mark Pendergrast, *Uncommon Grounds: The History of Coffee and How it Transformed Our World* (Basic Books, 2019).
3 Jeff Koeler, *Where the Wild Coffee Grows* (Bloomsbury, USA, 2017).
4 Sarah Rose, *For All the Tea in China* (Penguin Books, 2010).
5 Laura Martin, *The History of Tea: The Life and Times of the World's Favorite Beverage* (Tuttle Press, 2018).
6 Seren Cherrington-Hollis, *A Dark History of Tea* (Pen and Sword History, 2022).
7 William Ukers, *All About Tea* (The Tea & Coffee Trade Journal Co., New York, 1935).
8 Liam Drew, "The growth of tea," *Nature*, 566 (7742)(2019).
9 Muditha K. Meegahakumbura, Moses C. Wambulwa, Miao-Miao Li, Kishore K. Thapa, Yong-Shuai Sun, Michael Möller, Jian-Chu Xu, Jun-Bo Yang, Jie Liu, Ben-Ying Liu, De-Zhu Li, and Lian-Ming Gao, "Domestication origin and breeding history of the tea plant (*Camellia sinensis*) in China and India based on nuclear microsatellites and cpDNA

sequence data," *Frontiers in Plant Science*, 8 (2018): 2270. https://doi.org/10.3389/fpls.2017.02270

10 Gary Sigley, "Tea and China's rise: Tea, nationalism and culture in the 21st century," *International Communication of Chinese Culture*, 2(2018): 319–341.

11 K.C. Wilson and M. Clifford, *Tea, Cultivation to Consumption* (Springer, 1992).

12 I. Acosta-Alba, J. Boissy, E. Chia, et al., "Integrating diversity of small-holder coffee cropping systems in environmental analysis," *International Journal of Life Cycle Assess*, 25 (2020): 252–266. https://doi.org/10.1007/s11367–01901689-5

13 Fernando Vega, "The rise of coffee," *American Scientist, 96*(2) (2008).

14 C. Roden, *Coffee* (Penguin Books, London, 1981).

15 William Ukers, *All About Coffee* (The Tea and Coffee Trade Journal Company, New York, 1922).

16 Anthony Wild, *Coffee, a Dark History* (WW Norton, 2004).

17 R.E. Elson and Ary Kraal, *The Politics of Colonial Exploitation: Java, the Dutch, and the Cultivation System* (SEAP Publications Cornell University, 1992).

18 Erika Rappaport, *A Thirst for Empire: How Tea Shaped the Modern World* (Princeton University Press, 2017). https://goi.org/10.1515/9781400884858

19 Phillip Curtin, *The Rise and Fall of the Plantation Complex: Essays in Atlantic History* (Cambridge University Press, 1998). Doi:10.1017/CBO978051181914

20 Anne-Marie Feenberg, "'Max Havelaar': An anti-imperialist novel,"*MLN* 112(5) (1997): 817–835. http://www.jstor.org/stable/3251421

21 "Coffee," Fairtrade International, accessed 2018. https://www.fairtrade.net/product/coffee

22 Stewart Barr, Andrew Gilg, and Gareth Shaw, "Citizens, consumers, and sustainability: (Re)framing environmental practice in an age of climate change," *Global Climate Change,* 21(4) (2011).

23 Patricia Boaventura, Carla Abdalla, Cecilia Araujo, and Jose Arakelian, "Value co-creation in the specialty coffee value chain: The third wave coffee movement," *Journal of Business Management*, 58(3) (2017).

24 Jonathan Morris, *The Craft and Science of Coffee* (Academic Press, 2017).

25 William Roseberry, "The rise of Yuppie coffees and the reimagination of class in the United States," *American Anthropologist,* 98(4) (1996): 762–775. http://www.jstor.org/stable/681884

26 "Facts and Figures," Specialty Coffee Association, Accessed online, 2021. https://sca.coffee/research/specialtycoffee-facts-figures

27 Maria Uspenski, "Specialty tea – The Yin to coffee's Yang in the third wave," *The Tea Spot*, Accessed online (2019). https://www.theteaspot.com/blogs/steep-it-loose/specialty-tea-the-yin-to-coffee-s-yang-in-the3rd-wave

28 Edward Fischer, "Quality and inequality: Creating value worlds with third wave coffee," *Socio-Economic Review*, 19(1) (2021): 111–131.

29 Daniel Jaffee, *Brewing Justice: Fair Trade Coffee, Sustainability, and Survival* (University of California Press, 2014).

30 Mythri Jegathesan, *Tea and Solidarity: Tamil Women and Work in Postwar Sri Lanka* (University of Washington Press, 2019).

31 Debarati Sen, *Everyday Sustainability: Gender Justice and Fairtrade Tea in Darjeeling* (SUNY Press, 2017).
32 E.M. Reji, "Value chains and small enterprise development: Theory and praxis," *American Journal of Industrial and Business Management*, 3 (2012): 28–35.
33 Paul Hindsley, David McEvoy, and Ashton Morgan, "Consumer demand for ethical products and the role of cultural worldviews: The case of direct-trade coffee," *Ecological Economics* (Elsevier), 17 (2017).

2 Defining and Certifying Sustainability in the Coffee and Tea Supply Chains

The trend toward sustainability in coffee and tea has been catalyzed by the simultaneous global shifts in consciousness around the environment, equity, and economic justice.[1] The concept of sustainability, which decades ago was a revelation, is now firmly embedded in the lexicon. At this point, the field of sustainability science is almost a half-century old. Definitions have evolved over the last several decades and become more nuanced and context specific. One of the original definitions perennially referenced emerged from the Brundland report, which was published in 1987:

> *Humanity has the ability to make development sustainable, to ensure that it meets the needs of the present without compromising the ability of future generations to meet their own needs.*[2]

This broad and aspirational statement has left the space to determine exactly how the goal can be achieved and with what tools. Academics and practitioners have gone on to develop models and frameworks to create more actionable pathways to practice. One prevalent description of sustainability utilizes the tripartite concept of pillars, domains, dimensions, or spheres.[3,4,5,6] In this model, sustainability is envisaged as being comprised of economic, social, and environmental dimensions that overlap. This concept has gradually emerged over time that integrates economic, social, and ecological sustainability.[7] Depending on the context and evolving research, each pillar, domain, or sphere portrays areas of synergy that exist between the social, environmental, and economic aspects of sustainability. A shorthand overview of each dimension has been provided in Table 2.1 as a primer for the future chapters that will explore in more detail how this framework materializes in the context of the coffee and tea industries.

DOI: 10.4324/9781003228851-4

Table 2.1 The Overlapping Dimensions of Sustainability

Social	Economic	Environmental
The concept of social sustainability includes a focus on equity, inclusion, and human rights. This includes gender equity and the inclusions of marginalized groups based on other socially constructed concepts such as race and ethnicity. Social sustainability means increasing the participation of a variety of groups, particularly those who have been previously disenfranchised.	Economic sustainability is closely linked to social sustainability, and relates primarily to fair and equitable labor practices. It admonishes practices related to child labor and the exploitation of marginalized groups, and on the other side of the spectrum has a focus on increasing access to markets, providing a living wage, ensuring sustainable livelihoods, and improving financial support systems.	The more classic category of sustainability, which requires social and economic sustainability to be viable, is environmental sustainability. This aspect of sustainability focuses on resource use, from land to water to energy. Protection and conservation of green spaces, creation of zero energy, zero waste, and circular economic models are all embedded in this aspect of sustainability.

What does sustainability that integrates the economic, social, and environmental dimensions look like in coffee and tea? As many industries have attempted to integrate sustainability into their functioning, there has been a need to adopt a guiding framework that could address the multidimensionality of sustainability. In both the coffee and tea industries, the effort to integrate sustainability has focused on how to operationalize the three pillars in the context of the supply chain. This has included an elevated focus on improving the economic and social conditions of farmers, producers, and artisans while integrating environmentally sensitive practices. As the coffee and tea industries have evolved to integrate a strong focus on sustainability, the question of how to create change, and then measure and demonstrate impact has been paramount. This is where certification programs have become a key component of sustainability efforts across the supply chain.

To integrate sustainability, producer organizations, traders, and retailers have implemented and become affiliated with various certification programs. Sometimes, on one coffee or tea package, you may find a half dozen different certifications. These systems, whether fair trade, organic, or some other environmental social governance certification program aim to operationalize the social, economic, and environmental aspects of sustainability into concrete and measurable practices that are audited regularly by third-party verifiers. The goal is not just to communicate outward values to consumers, but to demonstrate their operational efforts through a logo. Often, if the producer organization has the administrative and financial means, they will try to gain as many certifications as possible to demonstrate the underlying commitment and dedicated actions toward sustainability. To understand what sustainability looks like in the coffee and tea industries, it is important to understand the processes and standards associated with the major certification programs that serve as pathways for achieving sustainability.

Certifying Sustainability

Certification programs have been at the center of reformation in the specialty coffee industry, which has permeated the tea industry and beyond. This next section provides an overview of the origin of the major certifications used in the coffee and tea industries. It provides a briefing on certification processes as a precursor to learning more from the producer and supply chain perspective in the case studies for this book. While there are over two dozen major certifications (and growing), the most common to emerge in the coffee and tea industry include fair trade, organic, and the lesser-known biodynamic.

Fair trade

In its modern form, the fair trade movement can be traced back to the late 1940s, where parallel models were developing in the United States and Europe.[8,9] Initially referred to as "alternative trade," the fair trade movement grew in response to poverty and inequity observed in the global South with a goal of providing not just a market for producers but also social services to politically and economically marginalized communities. Although the initial origins of the formal certification were relatively disparate, they coalesced into Fairtrade certification over the course of a decade between the 1980s and 1990s when coffee was integrated into the movement. Formal certification in Europe began first, with coffee and the private label Max Havelaar in 1988, and almost a decade later Transfair was created in the United States in 1998, the precursor to Fairtrade International. These independent labeling organizations set the standards for fair trade certification, and

in 1997 an umbrella organization, Fairtrade International, was established to coordinate the various definitions of fair trade across
national borders. The efforts of these organizations provided legiti-
macy to the fair trade label and helped to propel the movement
throughout the 1990s and early 2000s.

During this period, fair trade grew into a heterogeneous movement
that represented overlapping networks and coalitions of activists and
NGOs.[10] As fair trade was becoming more popular, the coffee and tea
industries were moving away from the first wave and into the second
and third waves, which promoted values at the core of the fair trade
movement. While the labeling standards have evolved, the focus has
been on providing a niche specialty market to small farmers and
producers. This is in an effort to assuage the inequities in the global
agricultural market while building democratically enhanced community resilience. Up to this point, the focus of fair trade had been on
supporting small-holder producer cooperative organizations. These
producer organizations would receive the fair trade minimum price for
their products. In addition, they would also receive an annual social
premium reimbursement that the cooperative could reinvest into their
community. This could take the form of additional technical assistance, establishing small-scale agricultural facilities, developing an
education scholarship fund for cooperative school children, or other
projects focused on health, nutrition, or gender equity. The most important aspect of the premium was that the democratically organized
cooperative associations would decide how to use the funds.

A widely accepted definition of fair trade is as follows:

> *Fair trade is a trading partnership, based on dialogue, transparency,*
> *and respect, which seeks greater equity in international trade. It*
> *contributes to sustainable development by offering better trading*
> *conditions to, and securing the rights of, marginalized producers and*
> *workers – especially in the South. Fair trade organizations (backed*
> *by consumers) are engaged actively in supporting producers,*
> *awareness raising, and in campaigning for changes in the rules and*
> *practice of conventional international trade.*[11]

From this definition, the broad-based goals of fair trade include six main
areas of focus. The first is to improve the livelihoods and well-being of
producers by improving market access, strengthening producer organizations, paying a better price, and providing continuity in the trading
relationship. Connected to this, but with a focus on distributive justice,

is the goal of providing market access to disadvantaged producers, especially women and indigenous people, and to protect children from exploitation in the production process. Another main component of fair trade is to raise awareness among consumers about the negative effects on producers absent of fair trade so that they exercise their purchasing power positively. Finally, there are several goals around promoting transparency, systemic change, and the protection of human rights by promoting social justice, sound environmental practices, and economic security.[12] These goals overlap with the three pillars of sustainability with a focus on the economic, social, and environmental practices of producers and their supply chains.

When most consumers think of fair trade, they think about the producers or farmers. But there are a variety of organizations that are a part of the fair trade movement in addition to producer organizations. These include exporters, importers, retailers, and umbrella bodies that bring together both producers and buyers, and retail organizations. Whereas consumers may just see a label on a package, behind the label lies a complex multi-tiered system of standards, auditing protocols, monitoring and evaluation, and assessment. Standard setting is part of one of the major industry structures of the fair trade movement. There are two original standard-setting agencies: the International Federation of Alternative Trade (IFAT) and Fairtrade Labeling Organizations International (FLO). IFAT, which is now referred to as the World Fair Trade Organization (WFTO), traditionally worked with craft producers who have sold their product through the alternative trade channels. These standards are continually updated and operate on a biennial self-assessment basis.

At the core of Fairtrade International's continued standards is that for a product to be certified, it must be produced by small farmers who are part of a cooperative organization. Individual farmers are small producers if they meet certain set standards based on the crops that they grow. For example, farmers growing fewer intensive crops such as cacao, coffee, herbs, spices, honey, and nuts are "small producers" if they meet the certain requirements. These include that they earn their primary livelihood from farming on a relatively small parcel of land, and that they don't hire outside workers except in certain highly labor-intensive industries, which includes tea. There are extensive protocols for fair trade certified producer organizations that have been outlined in detail.[13] This is a very labor-intensive process, that often requires significant administrative support to verify and provide evidence of traceability, sourcing, contracts, agricultural management, labor conditions, and a whole litany of other categories.

Traders are also required to be certified to establish a mutually beneficial and sustained trade relationship and to provide greater transparency. Just as producers must meet core requirements with added development standards, so must traders. Traders are considered all who buy, sell, or process fair trade certified products up to the point where the product is in its final packaging. This may take different forms depending on the products and their supply chains. For fruit, crops that may have a shorter supply chain, producers often label and package the product at their own site. This means the producers are certified as both producers and traders. In the coffee value chain, a coffee federation that unites multiple cooperatives may be a trader, in addition to a roaster that imports green coffee beans and then packages and sells them to retailers. Traders who want to become certified must comply with protocols outlined in detail in the standards guide for traders.[14] These standards apply to all traders who buy and sell fair trade products or handle the fair trade price and premium. The main components of fair and sustainable trading focus on ensuring that traders uphold the central mechanisms of fair trade. Broadly speaking, these include transparency of transactions that give producers at least the fair trade minimum price in addition to the fair trade premium, working collaboratively on sourcing plans, supporting access to pre-finance so that producers can fund their operations, and trading with integrity. This is all to say that there is an incredible amount of effort that goes into the certification process.

Perhaps the hallmark of the system is the fair trade minimum price, which is determined through producer data collected by fair trade organizations that estimates production costs. Fair trade maintains data on the Cost of Sustainable Production (COSP), which is one of the key sources of information that informs the development of Fair trade Minimum Prices. Fair trade Minimum Prices (FMP) are aimed at protecting producers from market instabilities while providing a safety net in case of low prices. COSP data is crucial. In addition to FMP, producer organizations also receive a Fair trade Premium.

As a result, the fair trade approach has gained appeal over the last few decades even though there are numerous critics of the system and certain areas for improvement. There has been a proliferation of a variety of fair trade standards adopted by different organizations under different labels. This represents both differing philosophical and logical practices, in addition to opportunity recognition on behalf of certifying organizations. In 2012, the movement confronted the largest divide to date Fairtrade USA became an independent organization and implemented a new policy called *"Fair Trade for Al"* which introduced more types of farms (such as large-scale plantations) into its certification system. Up until this point, while there were differences among the various labeling organizations, the underlying similarity was that to be certified the producer organization had to be considered a small-holder organization comprised of small-holder producers. This divide continues to shape the dialogue of power and politics in the fair trade movement amongst the growing number of certification programs and labels. While there are a variety of labeling programs that have integrated fair trade concepts into their protocols, the following half dozen labels represent the most popular that directly focus on fair trade (Table 2.2).

One of the original goals of fair trade has been to challenge international norms related to free trade. To achieve this goal, fair trade organizations have had to operate both "in" and "against" the market.[15] As such, there have been inevitable tensions. Is fair trade fair? Critics have questioned whether fair trade could ever be authentically anti-hegemonic, since it operates within the confines of market structures and does not challenge the ideology of consumerism.[16] Critics also point out further constraints to a system that supports lingering power asymmetry between the global North and the global South, a conservative understanding of empowerment by the movement, limited participation of southern partners, and the unequal distribution of responsibilities along the fair trade commodity chain.[17,18] Some of the main concerns explore the politics and power of fair trade.

The first concern is around the adoption of fair trade. While adoption of fair trade is far from being universal, the discourse of adoption within the fair trade movement suggests that alternative channels for fair trade should not be necessary. Rather, these standards should be embedded into the standards of all businesses. The false pretense of providing a consumer choice between "exploitative" bananas and Fair trade bananas would no longer be an accepted norm.[19] The second concern is around the assimilation of fair trade and to what extent it could be integrated into mainstream commercial trade, or if it would remain a small and lucrative niche. The latter has largely been the case where fair trade, like organic, has become a segmented product. Finally, there are justified concerns over issues of appropriation. Mainstream companies are increasingly using the consumers relatively weak understanding of the fair trade message to their own advantage. This results in "clean washing" or "image laundering." Mainstream business appropriating part of the fair trade message while altering or simplifying that message shifts the message from the exploitative nature of trade to the conventional problem of demand and supply.

Table 2.2 Overview of Major Labeling Program for Fair Trade Products

Fairtrade International	Also known as the Fairtrade Labeling Organization (FLO), Fairtrade International is the leading labeling organization in the United States. Based in Germany, FLO has both a certifying branch and a standard-setting branch.
Fairtrade USA	A nonprofit third-party certifier of fair trade products in North America. Fairtrade USA audits and certifies transactions between domestic companies and international suppliers to ensure that farmers and workers are paid fair prices and wages, work in safe conditions, protect the environment, and receive community development funds to empower and improve their communities. Previously called TransFair USA, it was a member of FLO but split from the organization in 2011 to allow multinational corporations running plantation-style agriculture to use their Fairtrade logo.
Fair for Life	Created by the Swiss Bio Foundation, the Institute for Market Ecology (IMO), and Social & Fair Trade Certification. This label is focused on human rights at any stage of production, and that small-holder farmers receive a fair share. Fair for Life is a brand-neutral third-party certification program. It does not use product-specific standards.
Equal Exchange	Equal Exchange was founded in 1986 as one of the original alternative trade organizations that helped to catalyze the modern fair trade movement in the United States. A for-profit company, Equal Exchange maintains an alternative trade model that utilizes direct trade, established long-term contracts, and offers higher-than-market prices to small coffee farmers. The company remains committed to supporting small farmers and producer organizations.
Whole Trade	Whole Foods, a large grocery retailer, uses a "white label" for their own stores called Whole Trade. They rely on third-party certifiers including Fairtrade USA, Rainforest Alliance, Fair for Life, and Fairtrade International. Products are co-labeled – for example, a Fair for Life certified banana sold at Whole Foods will also have the Whole Trade Guarantee label.

Ultimately, while there has been a significant body of literature that has criticized fair trade, there is still compelling research that has shown that these systems of certification have made changes in the lives of producers.[20,21,22,23] As the fair trade movement continues to evolve, more research and market-based analysis will emerge to distill the impacts of recent changes to the system. Interestingly, as a reaction to shifts and changes in the fair trade movement, a growing number of third- and fourth-wave coffee roasters and tea retailers have started to focus on moving to what they see beyond fair trade to offer what they refer to as "direct trade." Without a formal third-party verification system like many fair trade labels, this approach relies on the transparency of the business relationships and shortened supply chains that connect retailers directly to producer organizations.

Dissatisfied with the complexity and evolution of the fair trade movement, these new models continue to challenge the established fair trade system. Looking to the future, the overarching trends of both fair trade and the move toward direct trade highlight that there is an increased desire for greater transparency and fairness throughout the supply chain, from the producer to the consumer. Current policies structures and labeling practices are complex and arguably support very different visions for fair trade. However, with continued progress and transformation, they can continue to meet the original charge of the movement which is to improve livelihoods, promote development, raise awareness, enhance trade transparency, and protect human rights by promoting social justice, sound environmental practices, and economic security.

Organic

In tandem with the rise of the modern fair trade movement was also the rise of the modern organic agriculture movement. Systems of organic agriculture have been practiced for centuries, and there has been recorded evidence of organic farming methods globally.[24] The modern organic movement gave rise to a set of parallel certification systems such as fair trade, concerned not just with the specificity of techniques used in growing crops, but a more comprehensive scope of values. Alongside fair trade certification, many coffee and tea farmers also pursue organic certification. Today, a significant percentage of fair trade certified goods also hold some sort of organic certification, with USDA, EU, or Japan being the most common.[25]

Most of the modern written history of the organic movement and the subsequent development of organic certification traces back to early 20th-century farming icons in Europe and the United States. It should be noted that these histories reflect an orientation toward the West. They tend to ignore the critical contributions of organic agriculture traditions among indigenous communities that undergird centuries-old farming traditions of Asia, Africa, and the Americas. Those that led the way in the West to mainstream organics in modern agriculture include Rudolf Steiner, the infamous German creator of the Biodynamic movement.[26] Biodynamics is based on Steiner's book Farm Standard that captures key principles for sustainability in agriculture. This includes soil fertility management, crop protection, animal welfare, the use of organic preparations, and the preservation of biological diversity on the farm. Diversity in crop rotation and the preservation of farm fertility are at the center of biodynamics, which promotes the integration of livestock, compost, nutrient catch crops, and disease control through botanical species diversification. Essential to biodynamics is the development and use of nine different preparations made from herbs, minerals, and animal manures. Even before the modern organic certification programs began to develop in the west, the Demeter symbol for biodynamic agriculture was introduced and registered as a trademark in 1928, and the first standards for Demeter quality control were formulated.[27]

It was not until the 1960s and 1970s that the formal research and practice of organic agriculture expanded worldwide amidst the oil crisis, the counterculture revolution, and the modern environmental movement. As the organic agriculture movement gained momentum, a variety of standards were created at different levels of governance and from different sectors. There was a need for collaboration, which led to the foundation of the International Federation of Organic Agriculture Movements (IFOAM). IFOAM started as a platform for exchange. Today it has evolved into a platform for maintaining the Organic Guarantee system, working to harmonize and regulations and to advocate for organic agriculture at a worldwide and international level. Amidst 780 member organizations representing 100 countries worldwide, IFOAM has taken up the challenge of attempting to bridge the values of the founders and current developments in agriculture toward the globalization of organic agriculture.[28] Through consensus, the organization has established four main principles for organic agriculture:

1   **Principle of Health:** Organic agriculture should sustain and enhance the health of the soil, plant, animal, human, and planet as one and indivisible. Organic agriculture is intended to produce high quality, nutritious food that contributes to preventative

health care and well-being, avoiding fertilizers, pesticides, animal drugs, and food additives that may have adverse health effects.

2 **Principle of Ecology:** Organic agriculture should be based on living ecological systems and cycles, work with them, emulate them and help sustain them. Production is to be based on ecological processes and recycling.

3 **Principle of Fairness:** Organic agriculture should build on relationships that ensure fairness about the common environment and life opportunities. Natural and environmental resources that are used for production and consumption should be managed in a way that is socially and ecologically just and should be held in trust for future generations. Fairness requires systems of production, distribution, and trade that are open and equitable and account for real environmental and social costs.

4 **Principle of Care:** Organic agriculture should be managed in a precautionary and responsible manner to protect the health and well-being of current and future generations and the environment. Scientific knowledge alone is not sufficient: practical experience, accumulated wisdom, and traditional and indigenous knowledge offer valid solutions, tested by time. Decisions should reflect the values and needs of all who might be affected, through transparent and participatory process.[29]

Under IFOAM's broad, consensus-building umbrella, a variety of national-level organic standards have evolved. The most utilized and internationally recognized labels include USDA Organic, the EU Bio logo, and Japan's Organic Standard. While many other certifications exist, these often seek equivalency and may even use one of the internationally recognized standards alongside a national-level certification. Table 2.3 provides a summary of the major internationally recognized standards for organic agriculture.

All of these labels abide by variations of the same standards for organic production, which do not allow the use of prohibited substances, which may include conventional fertilizers, plant and pest disease control, and other chemical treatments. In addition, Recombinant DNA technology (GMO processes) are not allowed, and there are strict organic standards that must be maintained for cultivation sites.[30]

This is where the standards are operationalized, at the cultivation sites. Here, farmers are dedicated to implementing the rigorous standards of the organic certification. While some consumers may still be unaware of the specific implications of these labels, the rise of meaningful consumer awareness has helped to provide support on the

Table 2.3 Overview of Major Labeling Programs for Organic Products

USDA Organic Label	USDA Organic certification verifies that farms and businesses comply with the USDA organic regulations and allows businesses to sell, label, and represent their products as organic. There are three distinct labeling categories. 100% organic, Organic (95%), and "Made with" organic, which denotes multi-ingredient products and must have at least 70% certified ingredients.
European Union Organic Label	The European Union Organic logo can only be used on products that have been certified as organic by an authorized control agency or body. This means that they have fulfilled strict conditions on how they must be produced, processed, transported, and stored. The logo can only be used on products when they contain at least 95% organic ingredients and have further strict conditions for the remaining 5%. The same ingredient cannot be present in organic and nonorganic forms.
Japan Organic Label	The Japan organic certification governs products that are either **produced within**, or have final processing or packaging occur within Japan. The equivalence arrangement covers organic plant and plant-based processed products and livestock. Product labels must comply with labeling regulations. There are equivalencies with Australia, US, EU, and Canadian certifications.
Biodynamic Demeter Label	The *Demeter Biodynamic® Farm Standard* is a comprehensive organic farming method that requires the creation and management of a closed system minimally dependent on imported materials, and instead meets its needs from the living dynamics of the farm itself. Products <u>must</u> contain significant and verifiable Biodynamic ingredients to be allowed to use the term Biodynamic on product packaging and labeling, in order not to mislead consumers.

demand side for goods that are certified using social and environmental standards. There is a huge body of research that has explored consumer awareness and motivation to purchase certified products.[31,32,33] This research has confirmed that while many of the nuances may still be dimly understood by consumers, there is consensus that consumers are motivated to purchase organic foods due to ethical, health-related, and environmental concerns.

The pervading question of how to operationalize sustainability efforts is complex. Orienting efforts toward the overlapping three pillars of economic, social, and environmental sustainability provides a framework for ensuring that all aspects of human and ecological welfare and justice are included. While there are a variety of tools that can be used to implement, measure, and improve sustainability efforts in the realm of agriculture, sustainable business certifications like fair trade and organic provide a critical foundation. Like all human systems, these processes are far from perfect. But nonetheless, they provide an essential contribution that can continue to be improved. What is the most fascinating, and least understood, is the producer perspective on sustainability. The next part of this book will delve into two parallel case studies of farmer-led cooperative organizations that are both fair trade and organic certified. Both organizations also hold several other certifications. One is in Guatemala, the other is in Sri Lanka. They both represent examples of the evolution of the coffee and tea industries from their colonial origins to the modern third (and maybe fourth or fifth?) wave food movements. These case studies share the perspectives of farmers on the economic and social implications of fair trade for themselves, their families, and their communities. They also reflect on organic agriculture and their roles as stewards of the land that they farm.

Notes

1 Joachim Sauerborn, "Review of history and recent development of organic farming worldwide," *Agricultural Sciences in China,* 5(3) (2006): 169–178.
2 G. Brundtland, "Report of the World Commission on environment and development: Our common future." *United Nations General Assembly document* (1987): A/42/427.
3 Andrew Basiago, "Economic, social, and environmental sustainability in development theory and urban planning practice," *Environmentalist,* 19 (1999): 145–161.
4 Robert Boyer, Nicole Peterson, Poonam Arora, and Kevin Caldwell, "Five approaches to social sustainability and an integrated way forward," *Sustainability,* 8 (2016): 1–18.
5 Andrew Stirling, "The appraisal of sustainability: some problems and possible response," *Local Environment,* 4(1999): 111–135.
6 Koichiro Mori and Aris Christodoulou, "Review of sustainability indices and indicators: Towards a new city sustainability index," *Environmental Impact Assessment Review,* 32(94) (2012): 1–6.
7 Ben Purvis, Yong Mao, and Darren Robinson, "Three pillars of sustainability: In search of conceptual origins," *Sustainability Sciences,* 14 (2019): 681–695. https://doi.org/10.1007/s11625-018-0627-5

8 "Annual Report 2017." World Fair Trade Organization. Accessed online: https://wfto.com/sites/default/files/WFTO%20Annual%20Report%202017.pdf

9 Mukhisa Kituyi, "Fifty years of promoting trade and development," *International Trade Forum*, 2 (2014): 28–31. Doi: 10.18356/db1c4549-en.

10 Frederick Buttel and Kenneth A. Gould, "Global social movement(s) at the crossroads: Some observations on the trajectory of the anti-corporate globalization movement," *Journal of World-Systems Research*, 10(1) (2004): 37–66. Doi:10.5195/jwsr.2004.309

11 "Definition of Fair Trade," World Fair Trade Organization. Accessed online (2019): https://wfto.com/fairtrade/definition-fair-trade

12 Andy Redfern and Paul Snedker, "Creating market opportunities for small enterprises: Experiences of the Fair Trade movement," ILO, Geneva (2002).

13 "Fair trade standards for small-scale producer organizations," Fairtrade International. Accessed in 2019: https://www.fairtrade.net/fileadmin/user_upload/content/2009/standards/SPO_EN.pdf

14 "Fair trade Trader Standards," Fairtrade International. Accessed online (2015): https://www.fairtrade.net/fileadmin/user_upload/content/2009/standards/SPO_EN.pdf

15 Laura Raynolds, "Consumer/producer links in Fair Trade Coffee Networks," *Sociologia Ruralis*, 42(4) (2002): 404–424. Doi:10.1111/1467-9523.00224

16 Josee Johnston, "Consuming global justice: Fair Trade shopping and alternative development," In: *Protest and Globalization: Prospects for Transnational Solidarity* (Pluto Press Australia, Sydney, 2002).

17 Lindsay Naylor, "'Some are more fair than others': Fair Trade Certification, Development, and North South Subjects," *Agriculture and Human Values*, 31(2) (2013): 273–284. Doi:10.1007/s10460013-9476-0.

18 Aimee Shreck, "Resistance, redistribution, and power in the fair trade banana initiative," *Agriculture and Human Values*, 22(1) (2005): 17–29. Doi:10.1007/s10460004-7227-y

19 Will Low and Eileen Davenport. "Mainstreaming fair trade: adoption, assimilation, appropriation," *Journal of Strategic Marketing*, 14 (2007): 315–327.

20 Christopher Bacon, Ernesto Méndez, and Jonathan A. Fox, "Cultivating sustainable coffee: Persistent paradoxes," *Confronting the Coffee Crisis*, (2008): 337–372. Doi:10.7551/mitpress/9780262026338.003.0014

21 Daniel Jaffee, *Brewing Justice: Fair Trade Coffee, Sustainability and Survival* (UC Press, 2009).

22 Sarah Lyon, Josefina Aranda Bezaury, and Ted Mutersbaugh, "Gender equity in fair trade organic coffee producer organizations: Cases from Mesoamerica," *Geoforum*, 41(1) (2010): 93–103. Doi:10.1016/j.geoforum.2009.04.006

23 Loraine Ronchi, "The impact of fair trade on producers and their organizations: A case study with Coocafe in Costa Rica," *Policy Research Unit* (University of Sussex, UK, 2002).

24 Kumar Behera, Alam Afroz, Sharad Vats, Sharma Hunuman, and Sharma Vinay, "Organic farming history and techniques," In: Lichtfouse E. (ed.), Agroecology and Strategies for Climate Change. *Sustainable Agriculture Reviews*, Vol. 8 (Springer, Dordrecht, 2012). https://doi.org/10.1007/978-94-007-19057_12

25 Angela Browne, Phil Harris, Anna Hofny-Collins, and Ron Wallace, "Organic production and ethical trade: Definition, practice and links," *Food Policy,* 25 (2000):69–89.

26 Joseph Heckman, "A history of organic farming transitions from Sir Albert Howard's "War in the Soil" to USDA National Organic Program" (Cambridge University Press, 2006).

27 "Demeter Farm and Processing Standard," Demeter, USA. Accessed online (2021): https://www.demeterusa.org/learn-more/biodynamic-farm-standard.asp

28 Louise Luttikholt, "Principles of organic agriculture as formulated by the international federation of Organic Agriculture Movements,".*International Federation of Organic Agriculture Movements* (IFOAM) (2007).

29 Anonymous, *Principles of organic agriculture.* Accessed online: http://www.ifoam.org/about_ifoam/principles/

30 Japanese Organic Standard for Plant Production, Accessed online in 2021: https://aco.net.au/Documents/JAS/JAS_Standard_producer_1605_revised_2017.pdf

31 Gemma Harper and Aikaterini Makatouni, "Consumer perception of organic food production and farm animal welfare," *British Food Journal,* 104(3) (2002): 287–299. https://doi.org/10.1108/00070700210425723

32 Farah Shafie and Denise Rennie, "Consumer perceptions towards organic food," *Procedia - Social and Behavioral Sciences,* 49 (2012): 360–367. https://doi.org/10.1016/j.sbspro.2012.07.034

33 Hendrick Schifferstein, Alie Boer, and Mailim Lemke, "Conveying information through food packaging: A literature review comparing legislation with consumer perception," *Journal of Functional Foods,* 86 (2021). https://doi.org/10.1016/j.jff.2021.104734

3 The Rise of Guatemalan Coffee and Sri Lankan Tea

Introduction

On the surface, Guatemala and Sri Lanka couldn't seem more different from one another. Guatemala is a predominantly Catholic nation between Mexico and Honduras with over half of its population hailing from one of the 21 indigenous Mayan communities. Sri Lanka is a majority Buddhist island-nation within swimming distance of India that has a recent communist history. Yet, there are many surprising similarities. Both countries share the common history of colonization: Guatemala was originally colonized by the Spanish and Sri Lanka by the Portuguese, Dutch, and British.[1,2] Both countries also recently emerged from decades-long civil wars, which transformed the nature of social and economic relations. Agriculture is also central to both countries' economies.[3,4] In Guatemala and Sri Lanka, one-third of the population is involved in agriculture as their main form of livelihood. By comparison, less than 5% of the population in the United States and Europe fit into this same category. Each of these countries has also become well-known as a leader in the production of specialty crops: in Guatemala, it is coffee, and in Sri Lanka, it is tea.[5,6] This chapter explores the country-specific context for the rise of specialty coffee in Guatemala and tea in Sri Lanka.

Coffee in Guatemala

Coffee has been part and parcel of the volcanic Guatemalan landscape since it was brought over by colonists in the late 1800s to supplant the dying cochineal economy. Cochineal, which was once used as a natural dye to produce a deep ruby hue, was an essential ingredient to dye thread and garments in the Mayan and Aztec traditions. It became highly prized during the colonial period, with a robust market that

DOI: 10.4324/9781003228851-5

developed in Europe. However, once artificial dyes were introduced, the cochineal industry was all but decimated. Coffee came in to supplant it as a crop of the colonial elite, and it has been at the center of the Guatemalan economy ever since.[7] The modern coffee belt now spans the equator, and five of the top ten largest global producers today are in Latin America, including Guatemala. By the late 1800s, coffee had become Guatemala's primary export, and it has dominated the economy as one of the top three exports by value ever since then. Originally a crop of the colonial elite, coffee production initially relied on the exploitation and enslavement of local populations, many of them marginalized indigenous minorities. Some historians have implicated the exploitative legacies of the colonial coffee industry as structural contributors to the tensions that resulted in the violent and brutal post-colonial civil war. This period started in the 1960s and spanned multiple decades, officially ending with peace accords in 1996.[8]

The residual inequities of the coffee industry still shape the modern agricultural landscape in Guatemala today, which continues to have one of the most inequitable and concentrated distributions of land ownership in Central America. This translates into the long-standing landed elite controlling most of the productive terrain while maintaining concentrated political influence over agricultural land and labor issues. In contrast, subsistence farmers cultivate small parcels on comparatively unproductive sloping hillsides, primarily in the Western Highlands. Here, farm parcels range from 0.5 to 2 hectares (1.2 to 5 acres) per family. It is no coincidence that most of the indigenous population resides in the Western Highlands, which boasts the highest rates of malnutrition, poverty, and social marginalization in the country. Yet for smallholder farmers working the land on steep hillsides, coffee is still considered an attractive cash crop due to its value.[9] This is tied to the fact that the higher quality Arabica bean can be grown on high-altitude slopes of more difficult to cultivate agricultural land. Within the coffee industry today, the Arabica coffee grown in the Western Highlands is prized for its quality and terroir. This region is consistently ranked as one of the best coffee-producing regions in the world.

Guatemala is a very dynamic country, and I had the opportunity to visit numerous times over the course of my research. Even within the ever-expanding grid of Guatemala City, there are places of refuge with greenery, bike paths, and cosmopolitan city streets with a growing number of specialty coffee shops selling the country's finest beans. Antigua, about an hour's drive from the capital, enjoys a climate that is often referred to as "*La Primavera Eterna*," or the eternal springtime. It is no wonder this place has been designated as a UNESCO

World Heritage site, displaying cobblestone roads and colorful Spanish colonial architecture, wound around a quaint *plaza central*. Antigua's charming setting falls against the backdrop of a huge volcano called Acatenango, which at its base boasts one of the many coffee-growing areas in the country. The locals seem somewhat unphased by the steady influx of tourists, who flock to this delightful enclave year-round. On the weekends, even the *capitaleños* from Guatemala City would fill the streets of Antigua, dining, drinking, and celebrating. I spent significant time in the capital and Antigua conducting interviews and observing the evolution of the domestic coffee industry in Guatemala. However, it was in Quetzaltenango (also known as Xela, the original indigenous capital of the Western Highlands), where the coffee federation that is the center of this case study was headquartered.

The coffee federation is called FECCEG (Federacion Comercializadora de Café Especial de Guatemala). The organization had been created just in the last decade but it united eight different preestablished cooperatives from around the country. The growth and development of this federation have ties to the rising social entrepreneurship movement in Guatemala. More specifically, one organization with a focus on social innovation and equity, Alterna. Their social innovation incubator promotes the development of entrepreneurs from Guatemala who are focusing on solving key problems within the country. This group's mission was to support Guatemalan social entrepreneurs in solving these "wicked" problems. Their approach was not to import models from abroad. Rather, it was to incubate home-grown leaders with innovative business models that have a tangible and clear focus on improving conditions in their home countries. In my research, I came to learn about the founder of the federation, Juan Francisco Gonzalez Menchu, and his energetic group of cooperative organizations. With a mission of creating sustainable livelihoods for rural producers, FECCEG was established in the heart of the indigenous capital, Quetzaltenango.

The original rise of the modern cooperative in Guatemala can be traced back to the 1960s, when USAID and other international agencies began to prioritize rural development. In 1970, USAID approved a 23 million-dollar rural development sector loan for the development of cooperatives, and by the fall of 1975 20% of Highland Maya were participating in some form of a cooperative. By the late 1970s, participation had almost tripled, and of the member base, 60% were Highland Maya. Cooperatives have seen a resurgence in Guatemala in the post-civil war era since the 1996 Peace Accords. As of 2007, there were 729 registered agricultural cooperatives with 64,410 members.[10]

As institutional arrangements, agricultural cooperatives offer numerous benefits to members. Cooperatives can play an important role in supporting small-scale agricultural producers and marginalized groups, including indigenous minorities and women. In theory, they seek to empower their members economically and socially. They seek to create sustainable rural employment through business models that may be more resilient to economic and environmental shocks. In many cases, they also offer small agricultural producers a wide range of services in addition to improved access to markets, This may include improved access to natural resources, facilities, information, communication, technologies, credit, and training programs. Cooperatives also provide smallholder producers with the opportunity to participate in collaborative decision making. They can support them in securing land-use rights, and negotiating better terms for their engagement in contract farming. In theory and through this support, smallholder producers can achieve more sustainable livelihoods and can play a larger role in meeting the growing demand for food at the local and global level, contributing to poverty alleviation.[11]

In the modern global economy, cooperatives also offer another important benefit: they can become registered producer organizations through Fairtrade International. While the labeling standards for fair trade have evolved, the focus up until recently has always been on providing a niche specialty market to small farmers and producers. This is in an effort to assuage the inequities in the global agricultural market while building democratically enhanced community resilience. As described in a previous chapter, fair trade was historically envisioned as a development mechanism, with the focus being on supporting smallholder producer cooperative organizations. These producer organizations receive the fair trade minimum price for their products, and in addition they also receive an annual social premium reimbursement that the cooperative could reinvest into their community. This could take the form of additional technical assistance, establishing small-scale agricultural facilities, developing an education scholarship fund for cooperative school children, or other projects focused on health, nutrition, or gender equity. The most important aspect of the premium is that the democratically organized cooperative associations decide how to use the funds, as opposed to an outside NGO or international development organization.

While some of the cooperatives that had joined this unique federation in Xela were relatively new, some existed before the civil war started in the 1960s. As the civil war engulfed the country for decades thousands of Mayan farmers living in the Western Highlands, especially the Ixil

Triangle, went missing or were murdered. The consequence was a whole generation of families without their grandfathers, husbands, and sons. As a result, in a historically patriarchal society where men were traditionally in charge, women were left as the heads of the household. They became not only caretakers of the family but also of the farm and income. Out of the ashes of this devastation rose a community of women coffee farmers, many of whom were widows.[12] This created a historically synchronistic opening for women to occupy roles that they otherwise would never have had the need or opportunity to fulfill. As a result, a third of the members of this coffee federation are women, and in the Western Highlands, this number is often higher. This is why one of the lines of coffee that they produce for domestic and international consumption is called "Woman Grown," because those beans are sourced from the women coffee producers throughout the Western Highlands of Huehuetenango Department.[13]

Huehuetenango, or "hue-hue" as it is affectionately called, is home to some of the finest high altitude Arabica coffee. The cooperative that collaborated on this research, Comercializadora Maya Alternativa (COMAL), maintains an office just off the Inter-American highway en-route to the northern border with Mexico. The humble cement-block structure contained a few simple rooms, plastered with informational posters. At the time in the season when I was visiting for research purposes, the building was crammed with large sacks of green coffee beans. It was almost *Semana Santa* (Easter season in Guatemala) when I visited for the first time. The coffee picking and processing in this part of the country had just ended. This was a brief window of repose for the coffee farmers – between the coffee harvest and the start of the rainy season when the milpa crop cultivation of beans, corn, and squash gets going.

Here in Huehuetenango, one of Guatemala's three non-volcanic regions, specialty hard bean Arabica coffee is grown at the highest and driest altitude in the country. The term "hard bean" is a term used by the coffee industry to identify the harder and more flavorful beans that are grown at higher altitudes. The most common varieties of Arabica grown in this area include highly sought-after Typica, Bourbon, Caturra, and Catuai. The Huehuetenango region is unique, as it is characterized by a microclimate that is protected by frost, allowing the coffee to be grown up to 2,000 meters.[14] Due to the remoteness of this region, all the farmers must process their own hand-picked coffee. Once the coffee cherries are harvested, they are usually pulped in a hopper, washed, and dried in the sun on coffee patios. Due to the steep terrain, household roofs are often transformed into flat spaces for drying the coffee and keeping it safe throughout the process. The drying process is critical: if the coffee beans are not completely dried, this can spell disaster for an entire batch of beans due to mold issues. Once the beans have been properly and completely dried they are gathered into burlap sacks. Then, they are laboriously transported down from this impossibly steep terrain, through the remote hillsides, and to the coffee cooperative's headquarters on the Inter-American highway.

One of the coffee farmers I got to know during my time in Guatemala shared with me her view of how ingrained coffee has become in the national psyche. She said that Guatemalans, particularly Antigueños, grew up at the base of the volcanos where coffee is cultivated. Coffee is a part of Guatemalan life from early on. You can't really understand modern Guatemala without understanding coffee. The same is true of Sri Lanka with tea.

Tea in Sri Lanka

Even before tea was a staple export crop for Sri Lanka, coffee had been domesticated on its hillsides. Brought over initially by Arabic traders and pilgrims as early as the 16th century, coffee thrived in Sri Lanka until a fungal disease called coffee leaf rust destroyed much of the commercial crop of trees. In the 19th century, the first commercial tea plantation was established by a Scottish planter called James Taylor. Due to its huge success, the British established an industry of extensive plantation-style tea production, which replaced the existing coffee cultivation. These British-initiated tea plantations followed previous colonial models and were reliant on intensive manual labor for cultivation, harvesting, and processing. As a result, the British recruited many Tamil workers from South India to Sri Lanka as indentured laborers. They were unpaid and completely at the will of the plantation owners. These workers lived in crowded shacks, without sanitation, running water, medical facilities, or access to education for their children. When Sri Lanka became independent in 1948, the tea workers were legally designated as temporary immigrants. It was not until the 1980 that descendants of Indian Tamil indentured servants were granted Sri Lankan citizenship rights, although they continue to be amongst the most marginalized and impoverished communities in the country.[15] Formerly known as Ceylon, Sri Lanka has two major ethnic groups. The Sinhalese are the largest ethnic group comprising three-fourths of the population, with the second largest being the Tamils. While the Sri Lankan Tamils have inhabited the northern part of the country for centuries, during colonization a new population of

Tamils, Indian Tamils, were brought from South India to work in the tea plantations.

Although private tea plantations are still the norm and working conditions for the average tea plucker are still perilous, there have been significant changes. In Sri Lanka, these changes have created space for new models of not only more sustainable tea production but agriculture overall. During the 1970s at the peak of communism in Sri Lanka, land reform brought large estates under public ownership. As part of this reform, a large area of state-controlled tea land was distributed among rural people and the rest was brought under the management of two-state corporations. This moment in the evolution of the tea industry created the space for a new system. Public ownership was reversed in 1992 and regional plantation companies were formed which were sold to private ownership. However, some of the land remained under the cultivation of smallholder farmers. It was during this time that the cooperative movement took hold. While tea cultivation began as an endeavor of large plantations, with these gradual changes in the economy, tea planting in smaller land blocks has become increasingly popular and has led to the development of a smallholder sector in the country.[16]

Modern Sri Lanka is a pearl-shaped tropical island-nation with just over 22 million people. Although most of my time in Sri Lanka was spent in the tea-growing regions, I passed through the capital Colombo on a few occasions and found it to be a bustling coastal center with incredible diversity. A large portion of the population lives in Colombo due to its importance as an economic center, and you can find almost anything amongst the modernizing byways of the coast and inwards toward the serpentine city roads that lead out toward the rural countryside. I would often take the train from Galle through Colombo and to Kandy. Galle is a UNESCO world heritage site: a cobblestone walled fort that traces its unique placement as a bastion of commerce along the spice trade during the heights of the Ottoman Empire. Now, Galle maintains its unique architectural character while struggling to preserve its culture amid the frenzy of tourists angling for selfies along the walled coastal wall at sunset. Along the whitewashed fort walls, there are relics of the historic maritime tea trade. From Galle, the train meanders up the coasts rocking back and forth, with the salty crosswinds providing respite from the hot and humid tropical temperatures.

In Colombo, most passengers disembark as passengers from the capital heading to Kandy board in a frenetic exchange of bodies. While it is hard to beat the views of a coastal train journey, a portion of the interior train ride into Kandy passes some of the most spectacular ridges and jungle vistas on the island. Lingering briefly at quaint local train stations, vendors board to sell fried snacks such as dal vada and those of the fresher variety such as bags of rambutan fruits to the willing train passengers. As the train moves closer to Kandy, the climate changes significantly from the hot, tropical, coastal lowlands to the cooler and more temperate hill country that surrounds the city. Kandy is said to be the Buddhist capital of the country, with a majority Sinhalese population. Perched in the central hill country the city benefits from a more temperate, though still wet, tropical climate.

The hills around Kandy are where tea first got its start in Sri Lanka. Today, this is where several large farmer cooperatives in the Uva and Central provinces were united under the auspices of the largest agricultural federation in Asia. This new structure, imagined out of the possibility of post-colonial land reforms, offered a new model for the creation of a more equitable food system. In the early 2000s, Dr. Sarath Ranaweera, a passionate tea expert and proponent of organic agriculture formed Bio Foods Pvt, with a goal of working with a small team to help form regional agricultural cooperatives throughout the country. Part of the inspiration for organizing was to provide a well-managed strategic approach for small and medium-sized farmers to regenerate unproductive farmlands and to increase their harvest quantity and quality while gaining increased market returns. Dr. Sarath helped support the incubation of the first cooperative, by initially identifying and recruiting farmer leaders. These leaders mobilized their regional cooperatives and have helped embed organic agriculture into the practices of a movement that now represents over 24 producer organizations and 2000 farmers, half of whom are women. In my research, I was able to work with the Marginalized Organic Producers Association (MOPA), one of these energetic groups based in the famed tea-growing region in the hill country about an hour outside of Kandy. The group had been designated the "fairest of the fair" by the international Fairtrade organization. As a result of their collective work, and Dr. Sarath's vision, they continue to receive countless awards and accolades.

Surprisingly, although Kandy boasts several specialty tea shops, they appear to be outfitted more for the tourist than the local. The majority of teas on the shelf are first-wave tea bags, which mirrors the common paradox of cash crops such as coffee and tea, whereby the most curated specialty product is packaged for export. I was thankful to be gifted several bags of loose tea from the federation when I visited their headquarters in Kandy. They were just about to move their office halfway between Kandy and Colombo, to be better positioned to expand their offerings to the capital and export markets. The co-operatives themselves are organized around central meeting places in the tea-growing areas. They are situated along narrow dirt roads that skirt emerald-green terraces of rice paddies in the lowlands and tea terraces along the steep hillsides.

When I was visiting for research purposes, the meeting room of the cooperative which occupied a modest cement building at the junction of several unpaved roads, had been filled with chairs with a table set at the front for me and my research assistants. After a lavish greeting in which we were garlanded as guests with jasmine and marigold flower necklaces, we were all treated to aromatic black tea and local snacks. This included Helapa, a popular sweet served with tea and tiny finger bananas. Popular in Sri Lanka, Helapa is a traditional snack made with millet flour, treacle, and spices and then steamed in an aromatic Kenda leaf. While we shared the ritual of afternoon tea, we were able to discuss with the cooperative on the goals of the research, and the cooperative leadership helped to coordinate a plan with the group on how to proceed. After the discussion, we stepped outside and surveyed the tea terraces outside the cooperative's meeting space.

Once the tea is plucked on the terraces that surround the co-operative's office and beyond, all the leaves are transported to a regional facility managed by the federation that serves this group of farmers in the Kandy region. Unlike other regions where tea is plucked by the flush, in Sri Lanka the tea leaves are harvested year-round, due to the favorable climate. The tea leaves are all plucked by hand, which is an incredible feat, and much care needs to be taken in the plucking process. The raw leaves are then transported to the processing facility where they are dried or withered. Since the raw leaves are thick and waxy, they must be softened or withered for further processing. At this point, they are usually laid out to wilt, which reduces the water content of the leaves by as much as half. Bruising comes next, and this is where different approaches are taken to craft different types of teas. Oolong, black, and Pu-erh teas are usually bruised, which means they are rolled, twisted, or crushed to break down the cellular structures in the leaf and facilitate the oxidation process, which is the next phase.

Oxidation is where the leaves are then left out to wither for another round, and during this phase, the leaves turn brown. Heat and humidity must be controlled to ensure a consistent outcome. For green tea, this browning process is skipped entirely, as green tea is un-oxidized and remains green in color. To stop the oxidation process, the tea leaf is heated or "fixed." This step is applied to all tea styles except black, where the final drying step is used slowly to half the oxidation instead. Variation in heating results in different regional styles and flavors. Some are steamed, fried, or roasted and rotated in large drums. These styles of crafting can create endless variety, even within one category of tea. Finally, all teas must be dried and then packed.[17] As opposed to the coffee preparation process, where only roasting is usually done at a centralized facility, due to the nature of tea production, this makes collective organizing even more important for smallholder tea farmers.

Research and Methods

In addition to learning about the historical context and natural process of coffee and tea, a major part of my focus in Huehuetenango and in Kandy was to better understand more about the evolution of the coffee and tea industry through the farmers' experiences. What were their perspectives on sustainability from their respective situations as producers, cooperative members, and leaders?

As an outsider in both places and to both industries, I was fortunate to work with amazing insider research assistants in both countries. In Guatemala, where we were working in a very rural part of Huehuetenango, it was especially important to have insider research assistants. This is because the Mam language varies amongst Mam communities, but also because of the huge sociocultural divide that exists between urban and rural communities. In Huehuetenango, the research team was composed of six carefully selected assistants from the region, a few school teachers, a book-keeper, and a coffee roaster. Without them, this project would not have been possible. We all spoke Spanish as our language of communication. Ultimately our work with the farmers was conducted in Mam, one of the 21 Mayan languages. The majority of farmers also spoke Spanish, but we realized early on that the farmers would be able to communicate their experiences more deeply through their first language. So, with the help of this talented team, we worked to translate the research materials into Mam and went through team-building training before starting the work.

In Sri Lanka, I benefited greatly from a connection to the University of Peradeniya's School of Agriculture, where I was able to enlist a group of four enthusiastic graduate students studying soil science and organic methods. Typically focused on the technical side of the industry, the team was thrilled to get the chance to sit down with farmers and talk with them about their experiences. The students were all from agricultural backgrounds and had been actively working with farmers already as a part of their studies. As a result, they were able to connect and build trust with the farmers in their conversations. All the farmers we were working with spoke Sinhalese as their first language, and one of the graduate program's faculty had assisted in translating the research materials into Sinhalese for approval and use in the field with the farmers.

Each day we would head out to the field to greet the farmers as they arrived from their homesteads. As the farmers' stories from the interview process were transcribed and translated, we collectively learned about the complexity of the slow but steady institutional, environmental, and social change happening within the cooperative, and the deeper shifts that farmers were cautiously optimistic about. In Guatemala, we were able to talk with farmers from the cooperative, half women and half men. In Sri Lanka, it was the same. Some farmers spoke to us at length about their lives and experiences, while others, less used to the interview format, succinctly answered the questions at hand without diverging. Over the course of the research period, which took place in formal research visits that spanned from 2016 through 2019, there were periods of focused data collection with the farmers. There were also opportunities for site visits, observation during meetings, and attendance at industry expos. The research was focused on understanding the background and context of the cooperative associations and their work. How much did fair trade make a difference? Did the farmers identify with the concept? What were their perspectives on sustainability? Was this collective approach creating more sustainability in the industry? Part of the goal of this research was to better understand what farmers think about this system. How did aspects of the system impact their livelihoods? What were their daily experiences like? How did the systems improve their personal resources? What were their perspectives on their work as environmental stewards?

The next part of this book will explore insights from the farmers on sustainability in the coffee and tea industry. The first chapter looks at economic sustainability. It explores the extent to which cooperative organization and sustainable business certifications like fair trade have impacted the short-term income and long-term livelihood of coffee and tea farmers. The second chapter focuses on social sustainability and explores the extent to which certification frameworks like fair trade provide a process to improve individual capabilities and agency, collective empowerment, and gender equity. The third chapter explores environmental sustainability and farmer's perspectives on organic cultivation and their priorities as stewards of the land.

Notes

1 David McCreery, "State power, indigeous communities, and land in 19th Century Guatemala, 1820–1920," In *Guatemalan Indians and the State: 1540–1988*, edited by Carol A. Smith (96–115, University of Texas Press, New York, USA, 2021). https://doi.org/10.7560/727441-009

2 Sumedha Ponnamperuma, "Sonal Katyal, and Snajay Kumar Mangla," *Economic and Social Evolution of Sri Lanka from Colonial Rule to a Liberalized Economy* (PaKsoM, 2020). ISBN 978-86-80616-06-3 159

3 Edward Fischer, "Guatemalan political economies and the world system," In *Cultural Logics and Global Economies: Maya Identity Thought and Practice* (65–82, University of Texas Press, New York, USA, 2021). https://doi.org/10.7560/725300-005

4 Deborah Winslow and Michael Woost, *Economy, Culture, and Civil War in Sri Lanka*, (Indiana University Press, 2004).

5 Edward Fischer and Bart Victor. "High-end coffee and smallholding growers in Guatemala," *Latin American Research Review*, 49 (1) (2014): 155–177. http://www.jstor.org/stable/43670157

6 Kasturiratne Dulekha, "An overview of the Sri Lankan tea industry: An exploratory case study," *The Marketing Review*, 8(4) (2008): 367–381.

7 Michael K. Steinberg (Associate Professor of Geography), Matthew J. Taylor (Associate Professor of Geography), and Michelle Moran-Taylor (Adjunct Professor of Geography), "Coffee and Mayan cultural commodification in Guatemala," *Geographical Review*, 104(3) (2014): 361–373. Doi: 10.1111/j.1931 0846.2014.12031.x

8 Rubiana Chamarbagwala Hilcias Moran, "The human capital consequences of civil war: evidence from Guatemala," *Journal of Development Economics*, 94(1) (2011): 41–61. https://doi.org/10.1016/j.jdeveco.2010.01.005

9 Andrew Gerlicz, "Diversification strategies and contributions of coffee income to poverty alleviation among smallholders in Northern Huehuetenango and Quiche Departments, Guatemala," (2016).

10 Sarah Lyon, *Coffee and Community: Maya Farmers and Fair Trade Markets* (University Press of Colorado, Boulder, 2010).

11 *Agricultural Cooperatives: Paving the Way for Food Security and Rural Development* (Food and Agriculture Organization, Rome, Italy, 2012).

12 Ania Rapone and Charles R. Simpson, "Women's response to violence in Guatemala: Resistance and rebuilding," *International Journal of Politics, Culture, and Society*, 10(1) (1996): 115–140. http://www.jstor.org/stable/20019876

13 Alissa Bilfield, David Seal, and Diego Rose, "From agency to empowerment: Women farmers' experiences of a fairtrade coffee cooperative in Guatemala," *Journal of Gender, Agriculture, and Food Security*, 5(1) (2020): 1–13. Doi: 10.19268/JGAFS.512020.1

14 Christian Bunn, Mark Lundy, Peter Läderach, Fabio Castro-Llanos, Pablo Fernandez-Kolb, and Dylan Rigsby, "Climate smart coffee in Guatemala," *International Center for Tropical Agriculture* (CIAT), Cali, CO. 28 p.

15 Valli Kanapathipillai, *Citizenship and Statelessness in Sri Lanka: The Case of the Tamil Estate Workers* (Anthem Press, 2009).
16 Deepananda Herath and Alfons Weersink, "From plantations to small-holder production: The role of policy in the reorganization of the Sri Lankan tea sector," *World Development* 37(11) (2009): 1759–1772.
17 Saptashis Deb and K.R. Jolvis, "Review of withering in the processing of black tea," *Journal of Biosystems Engineering,* 41(4) (2016): 365–372. Doi:10.5307/JBE.2016.41.4.365

Part II
The Farmers Reform

4 Economic Sustainability for Farmers in Coffee and Tea

Introduction

As I walked up the road from my hotel toward the coffee cooperative's office in Guatemala, I passed small roadside advertisements for ferti-lizers, as well as shops selling materials and inputs to aid in the coffee-growing process. This was a coffee-growing country. There were sporadic hand-made signs indicating the price of coffee available for purchase, by the sack. Just before the cooperative's office was a small nursery specializing in the sale of seedlings of high-quality Arabica coffee plants. While the coffee season was ending in this part of the country, what had preceded this season of selling was the annual process of cultivation that captivates the attention, time, and resources of coffee farmers leading up to the arduous and yet auspiciously awaited harvest season. Before coffee trees can produce cherries, it takes years of care and maintenance. Once the coffee saplings become mature, which takes 3–4 years, the trees will blossom all along their branches with delicate white flowers that announce the impending growth of the green coffee cherries.

In Huehuetenango, this process usually begins in January as the coffee cherries grow and ripen. Once the coffee cherries are mature, they turn either a deep yellow or red, depending on the type of tree. They are harvested, processed, dried, and bagged in giant burlap sacks for pur-chase. The price garnered for coffee is governed by the intercontinental exchange, a major commodities market based in New York City where Arabica coffee is traded on the International Commodities Exchange at the *C* price. Like other raw materials, coffee is treated as a commodity and does not account for the production process, origin, or specialty status. In theory, the price fluctuates because of market supply and demand, without regard for the actual costs that go into production. If the market is flooded with coffee, the price goes down. Likewise, if there

DOI: 10.4324/9781003228851-7

is scarcity the price goes up. The buying of futures, the act of gambling on the stock market, also distorts the price depending on the whims and inclinations of those buyers.[1]

Tea has a different trading structure. The majority of the world's traded tea is sold through public tea auctions. These auctions trace their origin to the colonial tea auctions that were set up by the East India Company as early as 1679. While there were other auction centers operating, approximately a third of the world's traded tea came through the London auction for several centuries. In 1997 it closed. As countries around the world that were under colonial control became independent nations, these countries developed political and economic structures to manage their own agricultural production and cash-crop economies. Some of these systems were new, but many were built on the old colonial infrastructure that was left behind. The well-established model of the tea auction is one such vestigial apparatus that has been maintained.

Today, there are public tea auction centers in India, Sri Lanka, Bangladesh, East Africa, Central Africa, and Indonesia. These are all based on the British model of operation. Tea processors will work through tea brokers, who send out samples to buyers for price speculation, and then during the auction pricing is set through the bidding process. Unlike coffee, where commoditization has created futures markets that rely on a standardized price, in tea valuation remains somewhat subjective by comparison. Within this auction-based market, specialty tea continues to earn higher prices.[2] While there is transparency in the auction system as opposed to coffee, direct trade from specialty producers and processors has only recently been attempted.

Economic Sustainability

Economic sustainability in these industries is paramount, especially given the structural inequities embedded in these industries as a result of centuries of colonization. While extensive research has been conducted on environmental sustainability, less focus has been paid to economic and social sustainability, two concepts that are inherently linked. This chapter will explore economic sustainability, while the next will explore social sustainability. Economic sustainability in agriculture is tied to both short-term profitability and long-term stability. Economic sustainability for farmers is not just tied to the price that they can get for their product in any given year, but whether their farm and their form of livelihood can survive in the long term in a changing economic and environmental context. Profitability, liquidity, stability, and productivity are all traditional measures of economic sustainability. However, there is a more expansive range of indicators that have been proposed to capture other economic aspects of farming systems that are associated with sustainability.

Autonomy and diversification are two central indicators, beyond income, that overlap with social sustainability and characterize vital aspects of economic sustainability and long-term viability at the farm level.[3] These broader indicators that include autonomy and diversification require that farmers should not merely survive but thrive and prosper as a result of their labor.[4] Autonomy is envisioned as how economically independent a farmer may be. This could be viewed in terms of inputs, that farmers are less reliant on outside material resources such as feed or fertilizers and may therefore be less sensitive to input availability and price fluctuations. Autonomy can also be viewed in terms of financing, and the pressures from debts. Finally, diversification of income may also signal greater autonomy, as a farm's income can be diversified by implementing additional and nonagricultural activities such as on-farm processing, agritourism, and other similar opportunities. This chapter explores farmers' perspectives on economic sustainability and the role that both institutions and certifications play in strengthening their livelihoods.

At a basic level, income is key. In the coffee and tea industries, income is determined by the global commodities market. Farmers must rely on the ever-shifting balance of supply and demand, regardless of how much money it costs them to produce it. For example, in the coffee industry in the 1980s, coffee prices set by the entities like the Intercontinental Exchange (ICE) averaged the US $1.20 per pound. In September 2001, the market fell to a low of US 41¢ per pound, based on an over-supply of coffee, the lowest price in 100 years. The rapid expansion of Vietnamese and Brazilian coffee industries was partly to blame, with an excess in good quality crops that created a surplus.[5] Yet, it was the 25 million smallholder coffee farmers who experienced the worst hardships with every falling cent, while traders may have even seen significant profits.

This is why sustainable business certifications like fair trade have gained support. They provide stability for farmers who were otherwise growing cash crops that were and still are treated as commodities. One of the primary associations with the Fairtrade system, and the myriad of variations that have emanated from the original concept is a focus on fair prices for the farmers. Fairer pricing is a central mechanism of the whole Fairtrade system and the most widely understood at a high level. Pricing for Fairtrade producer organizations is determined through producer data collected by Fairtrade organizations that estimates production costs. Fairtrade organizations maintain data on the Cost of Sustainable Production (COSP), which is one of the key sources of information that informs the development of Fairtrade Minimum Prices. Fairtrade Minimum Prices (FMP) are aimed at protecting producers from market instabilities while providing a safety net in case of low prices.[6]

Farmer Perspectives

For farmers, income matters most immediately for their livelihoods. Being able to count on the fairtrade price, rather than the whim of the market, allows coffee and tea farmers some security in an otherwise uncertain industry. The farmers in both the coffee and tea industries shared that having access to better markets that would pay them a higher price for their crop through the cooperatives was essential. While they conceded that the difference in pricing was not that much higher, even a small increase for their farming labor was critical. The alternative in places like Guatemala and Sri Lanka is to sell on the street. In Guatemala, the coffee farmers referred to this as selling to the "coyotes." Similarly, selling to conventional buyers results in an undervaluing of their product. In Sri Lanka, the same was true, and perhaps even worse. Coffee farmers could process their beans up to the raw dried product and sell them directly to coyotes for sale on the export market. Tea farmers did not have the infrastructure or expertise to process the tea. They had to sell their raw leaves to be transported to processors who had the capacity to dry, cure, and prepare the tea leaves into a steep-able format. For both groups, joining a cooperative that was associated with a federation has not only given them access to better markets and economies of scale, but it has given them the ability to produce higher-quality coffee and tea and can garner a higher price.

One coffee farmer shared that he thought his peers originally joined the cooperative because of these higher prices. He explained:

> Well, we became members and it is because the prices of coffee were very low, but with the [cooperative] association there was a better price and we knew that the association supports small coffee producers.[7]

A woman producer also confirmed these assumptions as she shared her reasons for becoming a member:

I am involved in the cooperative to have access to a fair market for coffee and other products and because of its commitments to the women's association for development.[8]

Amongst the tea farmers, the sentiments were the same, where they shared that the profits from the sale of tea to private sector vendors and merchants was very low. Various tea farmers shared how they learned about the cooperative from neighbors, who divulged the higher prices they were being paid for tea. This was the primary motivation for most tea farmers. One tea farmer described their situation:

My life before was not good, we faced many difficulties as other companies who bought tea leaves from us did not pay much, they gave us a less amount of money. But now the cooperative is paying high amount of money for our tea, and it helps us to increase our living conditions. Now I can save some money in a bank account for the future. There were many financial problems before in my family, but now I can solve them with the extra amount of money that we are getting from the cooperative.[9]

It should be noted that none of the farmers spoke of the higher prices as a panacea for their situations. Rather, when confronted with the decision to sell independently or to sell as a part of the cooperative, the higher prices that they could count on from the cooperative ultimately made a difference in the stability of their income. Many of them commented that the prices were not that much higher, but that it made a difference. More than that, the farmers also shared that not only were they earning more through the cooperative, but that their income was more stable and that they have been able to save money, improve their household economic security, and build on their success by expanding their tea production and diversifying their livelihoods. One tea farmer shared:

My financial situation is more stable now that I am a member of the cooperative. They give us much higher rates for our tea than selling it directly to the factories. We can rely on getting at least 80 rupees per kilo of harvest even if the market is really low, because of the Fairtrade premium. Selling with the cooperative has shielded us from the unstable market, and this has helped to increase our standard of living. I have even been able to save money, between 500 and 1000 rupees a month.[10]

As a result of the higher income, farmers have been able to expand their production. Another tea farmer shared:

> The family income is more stable after joining the cooperative and I get more money. That money can be used for educating my children. I can also buy more food items than before. My living standard has increased, and I have even been able to buy 300 new tea plants after joining with the cooperative and I hope to cultivate those plants in the near future.[11]

Upon joining their respective cooperatives, the coffee and tea farmers shared that not only were they being paid a higher price for their products, but that they received other important benefits that helped to improve their financial stability both in the short and long terms. In the case of the coffee cooperative, one farmer shared:

> I joined this association because they buy our coffee and help us to find a market for the coffee and give training to help us create better products and how to manage the process, and they also give financial support in the form of pay advances before the harvest.[12]

Given the precarious and seasonal nature of farming, farmers may often struggle and even go into debt outside of the main harvest season. There is no biweekly paycheck in this industry. Thus, the critical financial support that cooperatives and federations can provide in the form of pay advances helps to equalize a farmer's livelihood throughout the year, when other subsistence income may not prove to be adequate to support their family. Another coffee farmer echoed this sentiment and went on to describe how membership in the cooperative has given her the ability to produce better quality coffee for the export market. This has resulted in an increased income for her family through livelihood diversification:

> Selling coffee to other countries requires a better quality product, which gives us more money to support the family, to pay for the school costs for my siblings. I am very happy to be a woman who is able to work on my parcel of land to produce coffee and that I have dedicated time to earn a living during the harvest and through the sale of my medicinal plants.[13]

Farmers relayed that the cooperatives as institutions have not just provided more stable and consistent income for the harvest, but access to other opportunities to safeguard and improve their livelihoods. In both the coffee and tea cooperatives, these institutions provided regular training on sustainable production. This includes workshops on composting, how to prepare organic antifungals, and they sponsored the distribution of other plants for livelihood diversification. One coffee farmer shared that it was through all of these benefits that they have been able to remain autonomous as a farmer:

> Through the Fairtrade initiative, the cooperative and the federation has given me and my family organic fungicides for Roya, medicinal plants, and fruit trees. These benefits that we receive help us to be independent "criollo" producers.[14]

With the tea farmers, this was the same:

> As a member of the cooperative, I have benefited financially, which has allowed me to spend more money on household improvements, buying food staples, and using some of the profits to diversify into pepper production.[15]

In Sri Lanka, one of the main issues for the cooperative was transporting harvested tea leaves. The farmers lived along unpaved narrow roads in some of the most beautiful and yet remote landscapes, with emerald green paddy fields reflecting the sky in their flooded pools, and up along the terraces with tea intertwined with spices. Another tea farmer shared how the cooperative has helped to avoid the costs and logistics associated with transportation in a rural area:

> This area is very rural, and there are so many problems with transportation, from the accessibility because of the unpaved roads, to the high cost. The cooperative provides tea collection lorries, and this has helped us as small farmers to avoid these transportation problems.[16]

In addition to Fairtrade minimum prices and the support of non-monetary cooperative resources, which are often a central motivator for membership, producer organizations also receive an annual Fairtrade premium that is disbursed annually to cooperatives. This premium can be used in any way that the cooperative chooses and many cooperatives choose to start education scholarships, feed the profits back into coffee production, or run other community-based health and education programs. In our discussions, some of the farmers reflected on how the annual social premiums that the co-op receives through the Fairtrade system have allowed the farmers to collectively improve their communities and access resources to support their families. In Guatemala, coffee cooperative members spoke at length about the community programs supported by the social premiums. The cooperative had used their social premium funds to start a school gardening program and to fund a decentralized system of small-scale composting production centers to improve the yield of their organic coffee plants. In the past, some projects established an education fund for the farmer's children, homestead medicinal herb gardens, a nanny goat program for household food security and inputs for fertilizer, and a bee-keeping initiative to aid in both pollination and income diversification through honey production.

As part of my research with the women farmers in Guatemala, we used the photovoice technique. The women participants were given cameras to take home to take pictures of their homesteads. We reconvened after three weeks with the developed photos and each woman choose three or four that were the most important to them to describe in a focus group setting facilitated by the research assistants. Through their photography and reflections, they shared some of the most insightful examples of how the support of the cooperative, combined with social premiums from Fairtrade has improved their household food security, livelihood sustainability, and pollinator presence for coffee farming. One cooperative member shared her excitement about the new honey project that they had begun and displayed a picture she had asked one of her family members to take of her checking on the honey supply (see Figure 4.1).

> Here I am working to extract the honey that we produce. Right now, we use it for our family's consumption, but through the cooperative we hope to find a market to sell it.[17]

Another cooperative member described the photo where she posed with her children, showing how she has been able to expand her income stream as a coffee farmer by selling coffee seedlings (see Figure 4.2).

> I took this photograph with my girls in the middle of coffee plants that I have seeded for my farm and also to sell, with the help of the cooperative.[18]

Finally, another cooperative member shared her experience gaining access to goats through the cooperative's programs. She described the various benefits to her household and livelihood as she shared the photo of her goats (see Figure 4.3).

This photo is of my goats. I received the pregnant nanny goat through the cooperative. Now I have five goats – I had six, but we ate one. The goats give us milk and more than anything, we use the manure to fertilize the coffee plants that we have.[19]

The photovoice data from Guatemala was especially rich in demonstrating the far-reaching impact that the cooperative has had in terms

Figure 4.1 Guatemalan coffee farmer and cooperative member checking on the honey supply produced as part of a livelihood diversification strategy.

Figure 4.2 Guatemalan coffee farmer and cooperative member displaying coffee seedlings for sale alongside her daughters.

Figure 4.3 Guatemalan coffee farmer and cooperative member's nanny goat and baby goats that provide material for organic fertilizer, milk, and meat.

of improving income, autonomy, and diversification. When triangu-
lated with the interviews, it is clear that this has certainly been the case.

In terms of economic sustainability, the main insights that the
farmers shared were important. Cooperative membership offered them
several essential tools for improving their autonomy and diversification, while also aiding in their short-term earnings. First and foremost,
through the cooperative, the farmers unanimously agreed that they
were not just paid a higher price, but that the consistency and relia-
bility of the cooperative's buying patterns allowed them to have more
stable financial realities. Some mentioned they were finally able to save
money and plan for the future. While the nominal increase in price for
their tea or coffee does matter, ultimately the stability and consistency of
the market mediated by the cooperatives and their federations were
incredibly important for farmers. In addition to the short-term economic gains, farmers also emphasized the benefits of being able to diversify their livelihoods by expanding their farming businesses and
developing additional income streams. Whether it was expanding their
tea acreage, or branching out to sell coffee saplings, honey, or medicinal
plants, the ability to embed security through multiple income sources
allowed farmers to have more control over their financial health in the
long term.

All these activities simultaneously improve economic sustainability
for farmers who become cooperative members. Institutional support
has been very important for improving farmers' economic sustainability. Linked to this support has been the overarching framework of
Fairtrade, which has created a niche specialty market for smallholder
farmers. The economic mechanisms embedded in the Fairtrade system
enable several of the key financial benefits that farmers mentioned in
our conversations. What mattered most to the farmers was that they
were empowered to decide and that they had ultimate autonomy over
how to use the funds. Through our conversations, they shared that
with the cooperative's support and the benefit of the Fairtrade social
premium, they were able to not only improve their own situations and
their households, but they were able to work together to improve their
communities using the annual social premiums. The next chapter explores farmers' perspectives on social sustainability.

Notes

1 Seth Petchers and Shayna Harris, "The roots of the coffee crisis,"
 *Confronting the Coffee Crisis: Fair Trade, Sustainable Livelihoods and
 Ecosystems in Mexico and Central America* (MIT Press, 2008).

2 Sarah Besky, *Tasting Qualities: The Past and Future of Tea* (University of California Press, 2020).
3 Laura Latruffe, Ambre Diazabakana, Christian Bockstaller, Yann Desjeux, John Finn, Edel Kelly, Mary Ryan, and Sandra Uthes, "Measurement of sustainability in agriculture: A review of indicators," *Studies in Agricultural Economics*, 118(3) (2016): 123–130.
4 Nora Van Cauwenbergh, K. Biala, Charles Bielders, V. Brouckaert, L. Franchois, V. Cidad, Martin Hermy, Erik Mathijs, Bart Muys, J. Reijnders, Xavier Sauvenier, J. Valckx, Marnik Vanclooster, B. Van der Veken, Erwin Wauters, and Alain Peeters, "SAFE—A hierarchical framework for assessing the sustainability of agricultural systems," *Agriculture Ecosystems & Environment*, 120 (2007): 229–242. 10.1016/j.agee.2006.09.006
5 John Baffes, Brian Lewin, and Panos Varangis, *Coffee: Market Setting and Policies. Global Agricultural Trade and Developing Countries* (The World Bank, 2005).
6 Raluca Dragusanu, Daniele Giovannucci, and Nathan Nunn, "The Economics of Fair Trade," *Journal of Economic Perspectives,* 28(3) (2014): 217–236.
7 Interview Participant 16. 2017. Anonymous coffee farmer, Cooperative Association in Huehuetenango, Guatemala, in discussion with the author. March. Transcript available upon request.
8 Interview Participant 3. 2017. Anonymous coffee farmer, Cooperative Association in Huehuetenango, Guatemala, in discussion with the author. March. Transcript available upon request.
9 Interview Participant 8. 2018. Anonymous tea farmer, Cooperative Association in Kandy, Sri Lanka, in discussion with the author. December. Transcript available upon request.
10 Interview Participant 7. 2018. Anonymous tea farmer, Cooperative Association in Kandy, Sri Lanka, in discussion with the author. December. Transcript available upon request.
11 Interview Participant 14. 2018. Anonymous tea farmer, Cooperative Association in Kandy, Sri Lanka, in discussion with the author. December. Transcript available upon request.
12 Interview Participant 22. 2017. Anonymous coffee farmer, Cooperative Association in Huehuetenango, Guatemala, in discussion with the author. March. Transcript available upon request.
13 Interview Participant 10. 2017. Anonymous coffee farmer, Cooperative Association in Huehuetenango, Guatemala, in discussion with the author. March. Transcript available upon request.
14 Interview Participant 20. 2017. Anonymous coffee farmer, Cooperative Association in Huehuetenango, Guatemala, in discussion with the author. March. Transcript available upon request.
15 Interview Participant 23. 2018. Anonymous tea farmer, Cooperative Association in Kandy, Sri Lanka, in discussion with the author. December. Transcript available upon request.
16 Interview Participant 3. 2018. Anonymous tea farmer, Cooperative Association in Kandy, Sri Lanka, in discussion with the author. December. Transcript available upon request.

17 Photovoice Focus Group Participant 5. 2017. Anonymous coffee farmer, Cooperative Association in Huehuetenango, Guatemala, in discussion with the author. April. Transcript available upon request.
18 Photovoice Focus Group Participant 1. 2017. Anonymous coffee farmer, Cooperative Association in Huehuetenango, Guatemala, in discussion with the author. April. Transcript available upon request.
19 Photovoice Focus Group Participant 4. 2017. Anonymous coffee farmer, Cooperative Association in Huehuetenango, Guatemala, in discussion with the author. April. Transcript available upon request.

5 Achieving Social Sustainability Through Coffee and Tea Cooperatives

Introduction

Each year, the federation of farmers from across Guatemala come together for their annual meeting. It was fortunate that I was in Xela while the meeting took place in 2017, and the group was kind enough to allow me to attend and observe. I arrived at the headquarters early and helped set up for the representatives from each of the cooperatives. They were making their way into a large room on the second floor of the offices right across from the roasting facility. As we got closer to the start time for the meeting the chairs began to fill. The corners of the room also began to fill with friends embracing after being separated by distance and the business of work and life. There was a mix of women and men representatives, and I recognized a few of the farmers I met on my initial visit to the cooperative in Huehue. In fact, several of us had coordinated to ride back to Huehue together after the meeting concluded. I was all packed up and ready for the fieldwork to begin.

The meeting lasted all day, broken up with time for a blue corn tamale snack in the mid-morning, and a later lunch. The full spectrum of the organizational topic was covered, from the budget to profits, logistics, and voting in new board members. The founder of the federation also gave a visionary presentation on future pathways for the federation. This presentation included insights into potential projects for livelihood diversification and even the potential for green building and agrotourism. Throughout the morning the federation also hosted an informal seed exchange, where folks placed prized seeds from their region: corn, beans, and prized vegetables upon the table. During the breaks, farmers gathered around to share stories about their varietals and discuss planting strategies. This meeting happens just once a year, and it was an intensive series of presentations, discussions, and collective decision-making. It was a long day, and by the end of the

DOI: 10.4324/9781003228851-8

afternoon the farmers and I were grateful for the chance to relax on the bumpy ride up to Huehue. The farmers from the cooperative who rode with me seemed satisfied: another annual meeting in the books. In fact, the oldest woman farmer among the group had been elected to a leadership position.

What does social sustainability look like for farmers in the coffee and tea industries? This annual meeting is emblematic of many of the ways in which cooperatives, in conjunction with certification programs, have built the infrastructure to support and grow social sustainability initiatives with their members. This chapter explores the farmers' perspectives on the social aspects of sustainability and how it manifests in the context of coffee and tea cooperatives. More specifically, this chapter explores the impact of sustainability certifications on various aspects of social well-being.

Social Sustainability

While the economic aspects of sustainability have been more robustly defined, consensus around the dimensions of social sustainability has been illusive.[1] Even the United Nationals Department of Economic and Social Affairs has had challenges in outlining this pillar of sustainability within the context of the United National Sustainable Development Goals.[2] While there have been many attempts, there is no unified agreement around the details, and each contribution to defining this dimension has been discipline and industry specific. In order to best understand social sustainability as it applies to farmers in the coffee and tea industries, a joint approach makes the most sense. A combination of the functionalist United Nations Sustainable Develop Goals (UNSDGs) and Amartya Sen's humanist Capabilities Approach provides some balance between population-level priorities and human-centered realities.

Across the 17 UNSDGs, there have been attempts to categorize the concepts to fit within the three dimensions of sustainability. Within the social dimension, the major themes relate to equity, health, education, housing security, and population. Each major theme is further broken down and delineated into subthemes with corresponding indicators. For example, the subthemes for health include nutritional status, sanitation, drinking water, and healthcare delivery. Each of these subthemes has measurable points, ranging from nutritional status to life expectancy.[3] In theory, this compartmentalized approach can help operationalize multidimensional sustainability through the vehicle of the UNSDGs. In some instances, this is possible, but in others it becomes complicated. This is partly due to the fact that there is significant overlap between each of the dimensions of sustainability, and all three together.

For example, economic and social sustainability are inherently bound together by the UNSDG that focuses on equity and poverty alleviation. These two pillars create inherently synergistic effects. Social sustainability is closely bound to economic sustainability, and it exists simultaneously at the individual and collective level.[4] The UNSDGs take more of a population-level approach. At the individual level, how can progress on social sustainability be observed and measured? More and more, practitioners of international development have turned their attention toward the ingenious yet simple framework of Amartya Sen's capabilities approach. This approach operationalizes social sustainability at the individual level. It embraces the connection between an individual's autonomy, agency, and skills as being central to their development and empowerment. Emerging research has begun to ask these more nuanced questions around capabilities that drive to the root of creating more sustainable human development.

These questions focus not just on resource distribution, but on the overall concept of human capability.[5,6] Sen's original framework of the capabilities approach poses: "the question is not 'how satisfied is this person,' or 'how in the way of resources is this person,' but rather, 'what are they actually able to do'." This is a more holistic focus for approaching social sustainability and human development. The perspective of a person's autonomy, agency, and abilities, rather than simply their assets and resources, is key not only at the individual and household level but also at the institutional and community levels.

Agency and empowerment are two key concepts at the individual level that are central to the capabilities approach and are embedded within the broader concept of social sustainability. Sen defines agency as "what a person is free to do and achieve in pursuit of whatever goals or values he or she regards as important."[7] Empowerment is a concept that is closely linked to agency. Various definitions of the term have been compiled and summarized by Alkire and Ibrahim in their 2007 study. They found that while there are variety of nuanced definitions of the term, empowerment can be described best as exhibiting two central components. The first component is an expansion of agency, or the ability to act on behalf of what you value and have reason to value. The second component of empowerment focuses on the institutional environment, which offers people the actual opportunity to exert agency to one's full potential.[8,9] Although agency uniquely lies within the realm of the individual, with empowerment, the opportunity structure (or institutional capacity) provides the necessary precondition for achieving one's full potential.[10]

Farmers' Perspectives

A focus of my research with the coffee and tea farmers explores how cooperative membership has shaped their lived experiences at the household and institutional level within the framework of the capabilities approach. How has participation as coffee cooperative members and leaders shaped the development of agency at the individual level and the dynamics of empowerment? How has this been focused through the opportunity structures of the cooperative and federation? Many farmers were initially motivated to join the cooperative for economic reasons. However, most members prioritized their continued membership for a variety of other social benefits at the individual, interpersonal, and community levels.

Farmers in Guatemala and Sri Lanka shared that the economic benefits and the price paid for coffee or tea was an initial motivating factor to join. However, they continue to participate in the cooperative because of the access it provides to education, training, and technical assistance. In both Guatemala and Sri Lanka, this was the same. One of the women farmers, hailing from the furthest distance in the neighboring department of Colotenengo in Guatemala, shared more about her experience in the cooperative:

> When I started participating in the cooperative it was for my personal development, my family's development, and the development of other families that are also small coffee producers. Because as a member of the cooperative I receive a lot of benefits, including a good price for my coffee, but also opportunities like mini projects, and training on important topics related to taking care of coffee so that I can produce good quality coffee.[11]

In Sri Lanka, this sentiment was echoed as well. A newer tea farmer shared that they joined the cooperative to improve their knowledge about tea farming and organic methods:

> I have many more benefits from the tea cooperative in addition to income. They conduct training programs and workshops regarding how to maintain plantation, planting, plucking, fertilizer application. I have participated in them, and they gave me a sound knowledge on tea cultivation.[12]

Socially, the cooperatives have also served as a gathering place for farmers working in otherwise isolated rural hamlets. Through the cooperative, they have been able to come together, share their own experiences, and learn to improve their cultivation practices through formal training and peer learning. In both cases, part of the educational benefit has been focused on improving their practices as farmers. One of the farmers in Guatemala shared how he got involved and why he continues to participate:

> I heard positive information about the cooperative's work both in commercialization and technical assistance. It is good for me to participate. I learn something and I have the ability to put what I learn into practice ... I do not care about losing a day on my farm to go and listen to the talks.[13]

In Sri Lanka, smallholder tea production is still a new endeavor. Early-stage tea producers shared how they have greatly benefited from the educational opportunities they have gained through the cooperative. One new tea farmer explained:

> The cooperative has introduced correct technical methods for plucking and pruning the tea, which has helped me to maintain a proper tea garden. They have also given trainings about the how to create and use organic fertilizers in the field. I have been using these organic fertilizers since the training and it has helped to increase the productivity of my farm.[14]

In both cases, the farmers also mentioned the importance of attending meetings, not only to benefit from the technical content but to connect with their community of peers. A woman cooperative member in Guatemala shared her unique perspective. Women have not historically been included, nor have they been able to attend functions outside the home. She applauded the cooperative in her comment:

> The cooperative gives us a lot of motivation – they give trainings and workshops so that we women can learn more and learn new skills.[15]

Similarly, in Sri Lanka, the cooperative hosts a variety of educational programming focused on farming practices, as well as management and access to other resources. One farmer shared:

Non-monetary benefits by the tea cooperative are organizing awareness programs, workshops about farming methods, and how to use compost effectively.[16]

In addition to education and training to improve their individual capacities as farmers, the cooperative members also shared how the cooperative is helping them at the household level to improve household food security and nutrition.[17] In Guatemala, one cooperative member shared:

> My most important experience has been through the trainings that I have been able to attend where I have been exposed to many new ideas and given seeds to plant my own family garden so that I can help provide a better diet for my family.[18]

A farmer from Sri Lanka also described how they began to integrate organic farming in their home garden, through the support of the cooperative:

> I got training for land preparation, to produce compost in my home garden, how to apply organic fertilizer, pruning, and weeding. I now know how to prepare compost in my home garden. Organic farming for my family is an environmentally friendly method, and my family will have less health problems and be able to eat vegetables with higher nutritional value.[19]

At this point, it is difficult, perhaps impossible, to disentangle the benefit of cooperative membership and Fairtrade certification. While the cooperative itself offers its own set of benefits, so much of what the farmers valued was tied directly to the protocols and programs of the Fairtrade system. Through the Fairtrade International certification program, cooperative members also agree to follow a litany of standards and protocols. These range from fair labor practices, to gender equity, and anti-discrimination principles.[20] All of these standards go above and beyond "business as usual" in commodity agriculture and are enforced through annual reporting and sporadic auditing and verification procedures.

Social Sustainability Focus: Gender Equity

An important component of Fairtrade certification also requires certifying producer organizations to demonstrate a commitment to, and action toward, gender equity and inclusivity. In both Sri Lanka and Guatemala, women and men cooperative members worked together as equal members. In both Guatemala and Sri Lanka, one-third of co-operative members in the agricultural federations were women, and in some instances women also held key leadership roles. However, in Guatemala, this has meant more proactively promoting gender sensi-tization within the cooperative with a focus on gender equity and empowerment. In fact, the cooperative even produces a line of coffee labeled as "Woman Grown." They embed gender equity into the federation and its cooperatives through annual trainings and work-shops. A key part of the focus on social sustainability in agriculture requires a focus on gender. This is particularly important in agri-culture, as more women are taking on formal roles in agricultural cash crop industries such as coffee and tea.[21] My research in Guatemala took a deep dive into the process of gender transformative change. This has been occurring through the integration of women into the cooperative, and the proactive strategic integration of women into the cooperative and the federation as part of their Fairtrade activities.

On my first official research trip to the coffee headquarters in Xela, the community partnership director from the coffee federation was kind enough to pick me up on the first morning I was to visit the coffee fed-eration. She arrived in her truck and after the paved roads of the Xela city center turned into dirt roads on the outskirts of the urban sprawl, we had arrived at the coffee federation's offices. The offices occupied the second floor of a building adjacent to the roastery. The headquarters were in a still undeveloped and surprisingly bucolic part of Xela. We arrived at the federation's offices, and as coincidence would have it, they were hosting a young women's leadership workshop for cooperative members that day. The workshop was facilitated by a Swedish NGO, We Effect.

The women were gathered in a large meeting room with chairs, where they were seated in a stunning variety of *huipil* and *cortes*, the traditional Mayan dress. The *huipil,* or top, is a box-shaped pullover with large open sleeves that have been delicately embroidered with different pat-terns based on the region of origin. In some places, there are distinctive flower patterns, in others there are animals. Some create mesmerizing geometric shapes and designs, while others are more uncomplicated in comparison and have simple lines woven into the fabric. The *corte* is the wrap skirt on the bottom, that can vary from plain black or indigo to day-glow plaid with silver and gold threading. The top and the bottom pieces are then brought together with a wide embroidered belt that unifies the whole ensemble and keeps the *huipil* in place. In addition to representing the diversity of Mayan groups, this gathering of women also represented select woman leaders from their communities. Although I had originally come for a tour of the coffee bodega, this session was infinitely more engaging.

The women were led through a series of activities where they were asked to think about their lives now and what they have, and to imagine what they want for themselves and their families in the future. Drawings were created by each woman of what she has, and then a second set of drawings depicting what she wants. Some drawings depicted upgrading their house from mud to cement or putting in a wood floor over the dirt floor. Some dreamed of increasing their property so that they could produce more coffee, others wanted to diversify what they grew or to take on livestock for extra income and nutrition for their families. Then, they learned various financial planning activities so that they could realize these dreams by saving and strategizing, with the training to justify why.

Following this session, the mood shifted, and the NGO facilitated a more delicate exploration of gender norms at the family level through the vehicle of improvisational theater. The women were split into two groups based on the following premise: a woman coffee producer wants to attend a workshop outside the family home to learn more about producing high-quality coffee. The first group was supposed to show a woman being subservient to her husband and family when they refused her permission. The second group was supposed to show a woman standing up for herself and giving explanations as to why this would be beneficial. Not only did the women put together fascinating charades in a matter of minutes, but they did so with humor and grace. They all knew the realities of how women are constrained in the home in traditional rural Guatemala. At the same time given their membership in the cooperative, they realize the importance of their contribution, not just as wives and mothers but as farmers and leaders.

The women members in Guatemala shared that they had particularly benefited from trainings focused on women's empowerment and leadership. These trainings had given them the space to grow and develop, not only as cooperative members and leaders, but as more vocal and self-confident members of their households. At the same time, men have also had access to trainings and workshops focused on the topic of gender, teaching the importance of new masculinity which embraces gender equity. This, in place of *machismo,* which has been defined in Latinx culture as strong or aggressive masculine authority coupled with female subservience.

Both men and women coffee farmers discussed the challenges involved in women's participation in the cooperative. Women are still often constrained by their husbands and cannot make independent decisions as a result. At the same time, they confirmed that slowly but surely change toward a women's more equitable inclusion is happening, albeit *"poco a poco"(little by little)*. One farmer shared knowingly, that this was not change that could be expected to happen overnight. Certainly though, women's participation in the cooperative has served as an important catalyst for shifting power dynamics. This shift is occurring not only at the institutional level but at the inter-generational level of the household as well. One farmer shared:

> I think every woman has the right to participate in organizations and to serve as leaders so that we can teach our children new ideas so that when they grow up, they will not be sexist.[22]

Although many referred to the importance of expanded opportunities for women within the cooperative, some farmers made clear that at the community level traditional gender norms still saddle women with the responsibilities for serving as the main caretaker in the family. Here, it is expected that they will do much of the domestic work, even as they have taken on additional roles as coffee producers, cooperative members, and leaders in the community. One farmer shared:

> Many women in my community want to take part in different workshops and trainings but because of their domestic work, they cannot attend. Many women do not have the courage to ask permission from their husbands to let them out and participate outside the home.[23]

At the same time, both men and women farmers agreed that women's participation in the cooperative was ultimately an improvement on the past:

> Each woman chooses to participate in the cooperative, just like for men. But sometimes husbands don't allow their wives to participate. But these men are "machistos" and they have not received trainings about the importance of the participation of women – but for me, it is great that these women are members because they enjoy and benefit from participating. Women have the right to participate in community activities, such as groups of women who participate on a committee. Not only men should have the power – and now our rights are leveling out and becoming more equal.[24]

Through their membership in the cooperative and the federation's formal trainings, women and men cooperative members have been formally exposed to new ideas while learning and interacting together in the context of cooperative meetings, events, and trainings. At the center of the slow but steady change has been the essential precondition of an enabling social environment that supports the expansion of women's and men's agency and abilities. The financial benefits of cooperative membership and the higher prices and social premiums connected to Fairtrade certification may have primarily motivated farmers to unite. Ultimately the farmers agreed that they benefited exponentially from the non-monetary resources that have helped them with personal development and social improvements in their communities.

Social sustainability in agriculture is a complex process that is not linear but rather is shaped by the interplay between an individual's capabilities, their relational interactions, and the presence of institutional opportunity structures. Embedding gender equity into an organization in the case of the coffee cooperative in Guatemala highlights this process. The organizational structures of the cooperative and the federation are critical in supporting social sustainability through the expansion of agency, leading to empowerment. In Sri Lanka as well, because of their membership, farmers have expanded opportunities to participate in decision-making as members and to develop their capabilities. Cooperative members gain knowledge, skills, and financial support that further increases their self-confidence and autonomy. Empowered with new knowledge, skills, and resources, they are then able to provide more resources for their family while improving their own lives as well.

Social sustainability in the context of the coffee and tea industries relies on nested institutional support for success. Since social injustice is embedded in society, creating change requires extraordinary effort to institutionalize and operationalize equity. Interlinked with economic sustainability, social sustainability requires attention at the individual and collective levels. This is where the cooperative and federation structures are essential, combined with the framework of sustainable business certifications. Since systems such as Fairtrade require proof of effort working toward social justice, collective structures must be embedded through the training programs and meetings of the cooperatives and larger federations. Opportunity structure is key, along with an enabling and supportive culture.

This chapter explored farmers' perspectives on the broader ways that the cooperative and federation support social sustainability. In addition, this chapter delved into detail around how gender equity, an elusive utopia, has been integrated into the federation in Guatemala. The inclusion and empowerment of women and men through gender sensitization training, an enabling and supportive culture, and leadership structures that elevate and provide space for women. As a part of their participation as members in the cooperatives they have received peer support, have been able to improve their capabilities through trainings and workshops, and have been able to cultivate an awareness of inclusivity and equity. The cooperatives are ultimately nested institutions that proximally benefit from their connection to larger federations. The next chapter explores how these structures support farmers as environmental stewards and share their perspectives on environmental sustainability in agriculture.

Notes

1 Margot Hutchins and John W. Sutherland, "An exploration of measures of social sustainability and their application to supply chain decisions," *Journal of Cleaner Production,* 16(15) (2008): 1688–1698.
2 "Social Development for Sustainable Development," United Nations Department of Economic and Social Affairs, Accessed December 7, 2021. https://www.un.org/development/desa/dspd/2030agenda-sdgs.html
3 "Indicators of Sustainable Development: Guidelines and Methodologies," United Nations, Accessed December 7, 2021. https://sdgs.un.org/
4 Ben Purvis, Yong Mao, and Darren Robinson, "Three pillars of sustainability: in search of conceptual origins," *Sustainability Science,* 14 (2009): 681–695.
5 Amartya Sen, "Well-being, agency and freedom: The Dewey Lectures," *The Journal of Philosophy,* 82(4) (1985): 169–221.
6 Martha Nussbaum, "Women and equality: The capabilities approach," *International Labor Review,* 138(3): 1995.
7 Amartya Sen, *Commodities and Capabilities* (Oxford University Press, 1999).
8 Ruth Aslop and Nina Heinsohn, *Measuring Empowerment in Practice: Structuring Analysis and Framing Indicators* (The World Bank, Washington, DC, 2005).
9 Anju Malhotra, Sidney Schuler, and Carol Boender, *Measuring Women's Empowerment as a Variable in International Development* (The World Bank, Washington, DC, 2002).
10 Sabina Alkire and Solava Ibrahim, "Agency and empowerment: A proposal for internationally comparable indicators," *Oxford Development Studies,* 35(4) (2007): 379–403.
11 Interview Participant. 2017. Anonymous coffee farmer, Cooperative Association in Huehuetenango, Guatemala, in discussion with the author. March. Transcript available upon request.
12 Interview Participant 11. 2018. Anonymous tea farmer, Cooperative Association in Kandy, Sri Lanka, in discussion with the author. December. Transcript available upon request.

13 Interview Participant 23. 2017. Anonymous coffee farmer, Cooperative Association in Huehuetenango, Guatemala, in discussion with the author. March. Transcript available upon request.

14 Interview Participant 2. 2018. Anonymous tea farmer, Cooperative Association in Kandy, Sri Lanka, in discussion with the author. December. Transcript available upon request.

15 Interview Participant 10. 2017. Anonymous coffee farmer, Cooperative Association in Huehuetenango, Guatemala, in discussion with the author. March. Transcript available upon request.

16 Interview Participant 8. 2018. Anonymous tea farmer, Cooperative Association in Kandy, Sri Lanka, in discussion with the author. December. Transcript available upon request.

17 Allastair Iles and Maywa Montenegro de Wit, "Sovereignty at what scale? An inquiry into multiple dimensions of food sovereignty," Globalizations, 12(4) (2015): 481–497. Doi: 10.1080/14747731.2014.957587

18 Interview Participant 14. 2017. Anonymous coffee farmer, Cooperative Association in Huehuetenango, Guatemala, in discussion with the author. March. Transcript available upon request.

19 Interview Participant 14. 2018. Anonymous tea farmer, Cooperative Association in Kandy, Sri Lanka, in discussion with the author. December. Transcript available upon request.

20 "Fairtrade Standards for Small-scale Producer Organizations: Fairtrade International (2019). Accessed online: https://www.fairtrade.net/fileadmin/user_upload/content/2009/standards/SPO_EN.pdf

21 Sabina Alkire, Ruth Meinzen-Dick, Amber Peterman, Agnes Quisumbing, Greg Seymour, and Ana Vaz, "The women's empowerment in agriculture index," *World Development*, 52 (2013): 71–91.

22 Interview Participant 8. 2017. Anonymous coffee farmer, Cooperative Association in Huehuetenango, Guatemala, in discussion with the author. March. Transcript available upon request.

23 Interview Participant 12. 2017. Anonymous coffee farmer, Cooperative Association in Huehuetenango, Guatemala, in discussion with the author. March. Transcript available upon request.

24 Interview Participant 17. 2017. Anonymous coffee farmer, Cooperative Association in Huehuetenango, Guatemala, in discussion with the author. March. Transcript available upon request.

6 Coffee and Tea Farmers Catalyzing Environmental Sustainability

Introduction

I woke up early at my guesthouse in Kandy and went around the corner to grab breakfast and a cup of tea to start the day. Balaji Dosa was a favorite spot, where South Indian and Sri Lankan breakfast items were served promptly with all of the accompanying chutneys and sambars. This was a necessary step before leaving to meet several federation staff at the tea processing facility in the hill country an hour outside the city. Since I was traveling alone, without my research assistants and our trusty van, I made the bold choice to take an autorickshaw up the twisty mountain roads. The fresh morning air was cool and reviving as we wove our way through morning traffic. We passed through the University of Peradeniya and the Royal Botanical Gardens, which housed centuries-old trees and an incredible array of biodiverse plant species. The trappings of the city quickly fell away and within 20 minutes we were in the more rural countryside, climbing the unforgiving hillside roads in the tiny rickshaw. The engine struggled to get around a few curves. As we approached a divergence in the road, there was a sign for the tea processing facility to the right and we continued up that way until we reached a gate. I got out of the rickshaw and unlatched the gate, and then we proceeded up the driveway past several large tea processing buildings to the main offices of the federation. The female security guard showed me up to a meeting room, where I was met by several of the technical assistance staff.

The staff smiled enthusiastically as we sat down for a cup of tea and discussed some of the origin stories of the cooperatives which grew into a federation. They relayed that the founder was a devout environmentalist and tea expert, passionate about human health and the impact of farming on human nutrition and the natural ecosystem. He shunned the use of conventional pesticides and herbicides and went

DOI: 10.4324/9781003228851-9

even further than the organic method by using the principles of bio-dynamics. Interestingly, many of these principles aligned with traditional ayurvedic approaches to farming that were indigenous to Sri Lanka. As a result, the cooperatives in Sri Lanka that were joined under this federation were not just certified organic, but they were biodynamic. The technical assistance staff were proud and eager to take me to see the biodynamic demonstration area where they were testing different applications of compost and other biodynamic preparations. They had a small building adjacent to the demonstration area where there were various brews and mixtures of prescribed biodynamic soil applications curing and fermenting. It was really inspiring, idyllic even, and their passion and zeal for this approach was evident.

Environmental Sustainability

Unlike the concepts of economic and social sustainability in agriculture, which have only recently been incorporated into the broader concept of sustainability, the definitions and frameworks around environmental sustainability in agriculture have been evolving for decades. The challenge of natural resource degradation in agriculture has been a perennial concern in agroecological research and sustainability analysis. Decades of research have sought to understand various aspects of this problem.[1,2,3] This research has spanned inquiry from how to measure the negative impacts of agriculture, to how systems can be shifted to adopt more sustainable practices.[4] Agronomists, behavioral economists, ecologists, and farmers have all been involved in efforts to re-align the system.

Although a variety of definitions have emerged, one synthesizes environmental sustainability in agriculture quite simply as "the maintenance of natural capital." However, this requires attention to complex processes that govern soil fertility, soil regeneration rates, and services from biodiversity (pollination, recycling, natural pest control).[5] An overarching pair of rules that define sustainability in agriculture include the output rule and the input rule. The output rule dictates that waste emissions from activities should be kept within the assimilative capacity of the local environment without unacceptable degradation of future waste-absorptive capacity or other important services. The input rule states that harvest rates of renewable resource inputs must be kept within the regenerative capacities of the natural system that generates them. In terms of nonrenewable resources, inputs should be set be below the rate of creation to ensure adequate supply.[6]

The environmental sustainability of agriculture has been on the international agenda for decades, with a more recent interest focused on mainstreaming organic and regenerative practices. Broadly, this movement has defined a sustainable food and agriculture system as one that improves soil fertility, protects the availability and quality of water and biodiversity, secures incomes of farmers and other actors in the value chain, and provides nutritious, affordable food. Perhaps most importantly, the flow of energy and the discharge of waste including greenhouse gas emission should be within the earth's long-term absorption capacity.[7,8]

Recently, the Food and Agriculture Organization of the United Nations included sustainable diets into the definition of sustainable agriculture, as:

> Those diets with low environmental impacts which contribute to food and nutrition security and to healthy life for present and future generations. Sustainable diets are protective and respectful of biodiversity and ecosystems, culturally acceptable, accessible, economically fair and affordable; nutritionally adequate, safe and healthy: while optimizing natural and human resources.[9]

While these definitions are useful for providing a framework of understanding, they are not immediately actionable. This is perhaps why sustainable business certifications in agriculture have filled the gap to provide practical guidelines and requirements for agricultural management practices that can be functionally implemented at the farm level. Environmental sustainability in agriculture today has become synonymous with organic. While there is variability in how organic approaches to agriculture are implemented at the farm level, the certification systems allow for some standardization.

The growth of the organics industry over the last two decades has been exponential. Current IFOAM data from 2019 shows that 72.3 million hectares are certified organic, compared to 11 million in 1999. In 1999, there were just 200,000 organic producers, and in 2019, 3.1 million from 187 countries. The organics market has grown in tandem, with market value at 106.4 billion euros today, compared to 15.1 billion in 2019.[10] However, there is still an incredible opportunity for transition, as currently just 1.5% of all agricultural land is certified organic.

Alongside the implementation of environmental approaches to agriculture has been a rise in consumer support of sustainable agriculture. Consumer awareness and consumer demand for organics have increased in tandem with organic production over the last few decades.

Research shows that demand for organic products is driven by the belief that such products are healthier and more environmentally friendly than conventional products.[11] When consumers see the organic label on a product, they may think about some bureaucratic institution stamping a rubber seal of approval on a carrot or banana. They may also have some understanding of what organic means: that it is healthier, perhaps more expensive, and produced without pesticides. The nuances and high level of detail that go behind the scenes are often misunderstood or glossed over. For example, many consumers still do not realize that if they are buying a USDA organic certified product, it is also by default non-GMO. Biodynamic, though more common in Europe, is even less recognized, and formal regenerative agriculture certification is still in the pilot stage now. Even with rising consumer awareness about the importance of organics, what consumers may not consider is what environmental sustainability looks like at the farm level. How do these certifications translate into knowledge and action? What motivates a farmer to commit to integrating and adopting these types of agricultural practices into their seasonal routines?

This chapter explores environmental sustainability at the farm level through the coffee and tea farmers' perspectives. In both Guatemala and Sri Lanka, the cooperatives and their respective federations produce coffee, tea, and other products certified organic through the US, EU, and Japanese systems. In Sri Lanka, the federation is also certified through Demeter International with the biodynamic certification. It was fascinating to learn more about the farmers' perspectives on these certifications, particularly the ones governing their farming practices and their relationship to the land.

Farmers' Perspectives

The farmers all had unique orientations to organic farming, depending on their own level of awareness and education about the method. There was a wide spectrum of perspectives, depending on whether the farmers were aware of and practicing organic methods when they joined the cooperative. For those that were new to the cooperative and had not yet converted independently, but did so when they joined, they expressed an initial skepticism and hesitancy around the risk of converting. There has been a plethora of research conducted in this area that has confirmed that the commitment to switch to organics can be an onerous one for farmers, fraught with risk and full of trade-offs.[12] In lower- and middle-income countries, this shift can be even more challenging, depending on what resources and technical assistance support are available. Some of the farmers shared their initial apprehensions about relinquishing the use of conventional pesticides and fertilizers, while others were anxious over the transition process. One of the newer tea farmers shared his initial mistrust of organic farming:

> I didn't have trust in organic farming, but then through the cooperative I learned how to produce and use organic manure for both of my fields. Now I have had really good results and I trust the methods. This style of farming has helped to increase my income, and I am really enjoying the methods.[13]

Although independent farmers would face these risks alone, with the support of the cooperative and the promise of a better market, farmers shared that there is more willingness to convert. In Guatemala, there was and still is a struggle to find a good market for coffee, and if a coffee farmer is not connected to a cooperative, or if the cooperative is not producing high-quality specialty coffee, which is often synonymous with organic, then it will be hard to get a good price. This coffee farmer reflects on his initial experience and why producing organic coffee has helped them:

> The price of coffee on the streets is very low and I was not able to get a good price but I wasn't sure about organic. Being a part of the cooperative has made a difference, and having the proper process for each harvest shown the benefit of organic coffee versus conventional.[14]

Some of the skepticism around shifting to agroecological methods was quelled through workshops, trainings, extension assistance, and peer learning from the cooperatives. A Guatemalan coffee farmer shared:

> As members we have a lot of things that we can share, including our experiences as organic farmers, and how we grow and cultivate coffee. One of the main benefits I have received from the cooperative include workshops, especially about how to prepare and use organic fungicides for Roya (coffee rust).[15]

A tea cooperative member echoed similar sentiments:

> Through the cooperative I got a lot of information about organic farming. Initially I thought organic farming would not be effective,

but the cooperative showed me that how to grow tea plants effectively with compost. I was having a big problem with rotting tea leaves, but the cooperative provided me with a particular biodynamic fungicide and now the tea leaves have totally recovered.[16]

Since the switch from conventional to organic can take time and requires a reorientation of practices and substitution of inputs and land management, it makes sense that some farmers may have been initially hesitant. When your main form of livelihood is at stake, taking such a risk can seem impossible. These farmers' sentiments echo those of other farmers who have made the switch. With the promise and support of an institution that can share not only resources but provide training and a guarantee of a better market, making the transition to agroecological methods were perceived as not only more palatable but ultimately more achievable.

Many of the tea farmers in Sri Lanka were keen to discuss their views on the global market for organics, and the connection between their role as environmental stewards and consumer demand. They were especially passionate about their perspectives on the important role of organic agriculture in the global food system. One tea farmer shared:

Organic agriculture is one of the major current needs in society, and it is the responsibility of us as farmers to produce foods without residual toxic elements ... that's why it is important to use organic agriculture as farmers.[17]

Especially amongst the tea farmers, where our conversations focused on agroecology and organics, there were strong perspectives on the de facto role of farmers in building a more environmentally sustainable food system. Many of the tea farmers also expressed their awareness of the connection between organic farming and health as it relates to the land, consumers, and their own well-being. One tea farmer shared their perspective on the bigger picture of their work as organic farmers:

Organic agriculture is very important for society. Farmers are normally providing food for society. So, farmers must produce foods without toxic compounds. So, it is important to use organic agriculture for farming.[18]

Another tea farmer echoed this sentiment, commenting on the important role of organic production in ensuring that food is safe for humans and the environment:

> Organic farming is good as health impacts are less. So, I think organic foods are good and safe for every consumer than using inorganic fertilizers. People tend to buy organic products as they are good to consume and health impacts are less. Without poisonous substances we can produce healthy food for consumers. So, it is good to produce organic foods.[19]

The farmers also shared their view of themselves as stewards of the land at the local level, where their agricultural practices have a direct and visible impact on land conservation, soil management, and the protection of biodiversity. One coffee farmer observed:

> Protecting the land is a huge responsibility of farmers. Because we are responsible for the land and the fertility of the soil. Because of this, I have been using strategies and advice from the cooperative to protect the quality of the soil and to restore the land.[20]

Many farmers were also concerned about protecting themselves and consumers by producing foods without chemical residues. One tea farmer shared the challenge that organic agriculture faces compared to conventional agriculture, where yields are often higher, and yet at the expense of human health:

> Agriculture is very important to produce foods without chemical residues.
>
> Farmers have a responsibility to provide safe foods for the society. These days' problems with food toxicity have increased. Farmers using chemicals to get highest yield. But the human health condition has reduced day by day due to that chemical usage. That's why farmers need to engage in organic agriculture.[21]

The connection to consumer demand for organics was also an important theme that farmers discussed. One tea farmer shared his perspective on farmers' roles as providers of healthy food for society:

> Farmers must give healthy foods to the society. So, organic agriculture is the best way for that. I think that consumers must

select health products. Then we can reduce the demand for products having chemical fertilizer usage. Then people can make a healthy society.[22]

A fellow tea cooperative member echoed this sentiment:

> Organic agriculture is important to reduce residual toxic compounds in food items. She said that it was better if all can engage in organic agriculture to reduce toxicity in foods for both farmers and customers.[23]

Many of the farmers also reflected on the role that consumers play in shaping demand for organic products. Several noted that there has been good demand recently in the market and that there is an increasing trend amongst consumers who want to purchase organic foods to improve health and nutrition. A tea farmer elaborated on this idea:

> Consumers want to purchase organic products as the health impacts are less by consuming organic foods. Unfortunately, sometimes people only realized they should use organic products after realizing that they have health issues. Consuming organics can help reduce health problems and give higher nutritional value. Right now, there is good demand in the market and a trend has started to purchase organic foods.[24]

The coffee farmers in Guatemala were also enthusiastic about the prospect of producing organic coffee for the growing market demand for organics. A woman coffee farmer shared:

> We are working with organic coffee and this has helped us to sell our coffee in other countries. Because in Guatemala the organic coffee is grown so that other countries will buy it and we work very hard to produce organic coffee to be able to sell better coffee in other countries. I feel happy to be a woman working in the coffee industry, and I have done very well as a member in the cooperative.[25]

In both contexts, the farmers were aware of the nested impacts of organic agriculture on their own health, the land, and the consumer market both locally and globally. While the export market has had strong demand for organics, recently there has been an increase in demand for organic consumption domestically as well.

Overall, the farmers saw themselves as active agents of change, and integral participants in the organics movement. Farmers were empowered through the collective strength of the cooperative as an institution and the federation that serves as an administrative center and conduit for connecting to the expanding growing market for organics. Key to this dynamic was not just the availability of training and resources, but also the interaction, peer learning, and relationship building within the cooperative that promoted trust, reciprocity, and collaboration. What was fascinating to learn was that farmers saw themselves as stewards of the land. Perhaps more importantly, they also saw themselves as connected to a broader movement that seeks to provide the market and consumers with healthy foods that would not negatively impact health.

In addition, farmers acknowledged an important environmental justice issue in agriculture: that since farmers are working directly with the inputs they provide to the land and their crops, they ultimately bear the costs of such inputs to their own health and the health of their families. Using conventional methods has resulted in documented cases of environmental degradation to the land, and individual contamination for farmers and farm workers.[26,27] To produce organic means not only to produce a higher quality product, a product that would garner higher prices, and a product that would be healthier for the consumer market, but ultimately a form of agriculture that supports the health of the farmers themselves. Once farmers had converted their commercial growing to organic, it just made sense to them to produce organic fruits and vegetables in their homesteads.

The ripple effect of converting can be seen at all levels of the system. This is something that is often an afterthought for the consumers, who are predominantly concerned about their own health. This has been changing though, with the availability and popularity of organic products, and the increasing concern of consumers about all aspects of sustainability.[28] Now, there is more awareness by supporting organic agriculture at the consumer level individuals are not only supporting the health of the land but the health of farmers as well. This is where the spheres of environmental sustainability in agriculture overlap considerably with the sphere of social sustainability in agriculture. In this way, organic agriculture supports not only environmental sustainability, but social sustainability as well. Ensuring that farmers are healthy, and not exposed to harmful inputs is a key measure of social sustainability in agriculture.

While cooperative members have more control of their autonomy as farmers, for farm workers and wage labor, organic approaches to agriculture create an even more significant impact on social sustainability at the farm level. With significantly less autonomy, and farm workers and wage labor hired to help with the harvest, both for the cooperative members in these cases, and in external environments that rely on large-scale cultivation and harvesting, this is even more critical. Even in specialty coffee and tea, cooperative members often rely on hiring wage labor during the peak of harvesting time, to ensure that their crops are captured and transported for processing. These themes were echoed widely in conversations at other levels of the supply chains that coordinate with the cooperatives and the federations. The next few chapters will explore how these themes manifest along the supply chain, and ultimately impact global markets in coffee and tea, creating a ripple effect to parallel agricultural systems and even industries outside agriculture.

The global market for organics continues to grow. In Guatemala and Sri Lanka, there has been a positive uptick in domestic interest in organics. Many factors have contributed to this shift, including an overarching growth of the economy. There is greater awareness, education, and purchasing power that influences local markets. As I was conducting research in Guatemala, there were several specialty shops selling organic produce and weekly farmers' markets in urban hubs that served as outlets for selling organic produce to the local community. Over the course of the pandemic, some of these markets even shifted to online ordering and delivery, a prime example being Cinco Azul. Cinco Azul, formerly La Botica Verde is a start-up founded by a passionate local in Antigua. This business began through the coordination of small farmers using organic methods to grow vegetables, many of whom had started out in the coffee industry, some cooperative members, who saw an opportunity to diversify and expand their income through local production. Through the power of the organics movement, this group now had an enthusiastic local market to support their supply and garner significantly higher prices than they would receive had they sold their vegetables solo amongst other conventional vegetable growers are municipal markets.

In Sri Lanka, the experience has been similar. With the growing demand for organics locally, the federation has coordinated with its cooperatives to produce an array of organic vegetables and products, in addition to organic tea. They launched a flagship store on the road from Kandy to Colombo, to capture both urban markets. Since 2020, the COVID-19 pandemic accelerated the demand for online ordering and delivery, and the federation was poised to meet such demand with a similar approach to Cinco Azul. Residents of Colombo can now not only visit the brick and mortar store, where they receive weekly updates on what is fresh and available, but they can also order delivery and subscribe to a regular order, inspired by the community-supported agriculture model. What has been most surprising and unexpected has been that the government in Sri Lanka has banned chemical fertilizers, in pursuit of becoming the world's first 100% organic food producer in 2021. While there have been significant hardships to this transition, exacerbated by the pandemic, the government is hopeful that the process will take just a few years. Although there has been criticism of the effort, which was imposed on farmers without ample support for transitioning, most farmers said they were supportive of the organic vision, realizing that it would require more than a year for them to make the switch. The government facilitated a survey to better understand the situation on the ground.

The survey found that over 90% of farmers are currently using chemical fertilizer, and almost all of them expect a huge reduction in their harvest during the transition. The most dependent farmers were those producing rice, followed by tea and rubber. Only 20% of farmers surveyed felt that they had the appropriate knowledge on suitable organic fertilizers and proper application and management of their crops using these methods. Through the survey process, farmers requested that the government provide advice and instructions on organic fertilizer, grant more time to make a gradual transition, and standardize the supply of organic alternatives.

Such a bold stance has evoked enthusiasm and also consternation. Shifting from conventional to organics for a singular product like tea is challenging enough, let alone transitioning all crops from conventional to organic. While Sri Lanka faces challenges in this revolutionary change, lessons can be learned from the farmers' sentiments. At the individual level, farmers need education, technical assistance, training, and peer support. This kind of transition requires significant and constant input from institutions, and likely subsidies and incentives as well. At the organizational level, cooperatives and other structures can provide not only technical assistance and education, but economic support as well, providing access to more lucrative markets for organic products. In both the case of Guatemala and Sri Lanka, the federations and their cooperatives have gone on to diversify their production of other organic crops and value-added products. These examples really highlight the importance of institutional support at all levels in helping farmers realize their goals of transitioning to more environmentally sustainable methods of production, whether voluntarily or by mandate.

Economic, social, and environmental sustainability in agriculture is embodied by distinct and yet overlapping spheres, that are pursued at the level of the farmer and the cooperative. Gaining access to the lives and perspectives of farmers navigating these systems is critical in understanding to what extent sustainable business certifications are impacting their lives, livelihoods, and the land that they farm. The last three chapters have explored farmers' observations about the economic, social, and environmental effects of sustainable business certifications including fairtrade, organic, and several others. In combination with their participation as members in cooperatives, the overall sentiment has been that they are able to get a better price, access more secure markets, receive trainings and workshops that improve their capabilities, live healthier more productive lives as farmers using agroecological methods, and cultivate and awareness of inclusivity and equity. The cooperatives are ultimately nested institutions that proximally benefit from their connection to larger federations. These federations are then connected to a global supply chain of exporters, importers, roasters, packers, and retailers. The next two chapters will explore value chain perspectives on sustainability in the coffee and tea industries and provide a 30,000-foot view of the dynamics of nested institutional support that reinforces and promotes increasing gains toward higher levels of sustainability.

Notes

1 Bekele Shiferaw, Julius Okello, and Ratna Reddy, "Adoption and adaptation of natural resource management innovations in smallholder agriculture: Reflections on key lessons and best practices," *Environment, Development, and Sustainability,* 11 (2009): 601–619. https://doi.org/10.1007/s10668-007-9132-1

2 Frank Place, Ruth Meinzen-Dick, and Hosaena Ghebru, "Natural resource management and resource rights for agriculture," IFPRI Book Chapters, In *Agricultural Development: New Perspectives in a Changing World,* Chapter 18 (595–628, International Food Policy Research Institute (IFPRI), 2001).

3 National Research Council, *Toward Sustainability: A Plan for Collaborative Research on Agriculture and Natural Resource Management* (National Academies Press, 1991).

4 Noor Sabhia, Ruhul Salim, Sanzidur Rahman, and Maria Fay Rola-Rubzen, "Measuring environmental sustainability in agriculture: A composite environmental impact index approach," *Journal of Environmental Management,* 166 (2016): 84–93.

5 Shailesh Yadav, Arnab Banerjee, Manoj Jhariya, Abhishek Raj, Nahid Khan, Ram Swaroop Meena, and Sandeep Kumar, "Agroecology towards environmental sustainability," In *Sustainable Intensification for Agroecosystem Services and Management* (323–352, Springer, Singapore, 2001).

6 David Pimentel, Laura Westra, and Reed Noss, *Ecological Integrity: Integrating Environment, Conservation, and Health* (Island Press, 2000).

7 Neils Halberg, "Assessment of the environmental sustainability of organic farming: Definitions, indicators and the major challenges," *Canadian Journal of Plant Science* (2012). Doi: https://doi.org/10.4141/cjps2012-035

8 Emma Soulé, Philip Michonneau, Nadia Michel, and Christian Bockstaller, "Environmental sustainability assessment in agricultural systems: A conceptual and methodological review," *Journal of Cleaner Production*, 129291 (2021).

9 "Food-based Dietary Guidelines: Dietary Guidelines and Sustainability," Food and Agriculture Organization (2021). Accessed online: https://www.fao.org/nutrition/education/food-dietaryguidelines/background/sustainable-dietary-guidelines/en/

10 H. Willer, J. Travnicek, C. Meier, and B. Schlater, "The World of Organic Agriculture: Statistics and Emerging Trends for 2021," (2021) Accessed online: https://www.fibl.org/fileadmin/documents/shop/1150organic-world2021.pdf

11 Donald Lotter, "Organic Agriculture,"*Journal of Sustainable Agriculture*, 21 (2003): 59–128.

12 Claire Lamine, "Transition pathways towards a robust ecologization of agriculture and the need for system redesign. Cases from organic farming and IPM," *Journal of Rural Studies*, 27 (2) (2011): 209–219.

13 Interview Participant 14. 2018. Anonymous tea farmer, Cooperative Association in Kandy, Sri Lanka, in discussion with the author. December. Transcript available upon request.

14 Interview Participant 2. 2017. Anonymous coffee farmer, Cooperative Association in Huehuetenango, Guatemala, in discussion with the author. March. Transcript available upon request.

15 Interview Participant 14. 2017. Anonymous coffee farmer, Cooperative Association in Huehuetenango, Guatemala, in discussion with the author. March. Transcript available upon request.

16 Interview Participant 10. 2018. Anonymous tea farmer, Cooperative Association in Kandy, Sri Lanka, in discussion with the author. December. Transcript available upon request.

17 Interview Participant 16. 2018. Anonymous tea farmer, Cooperative Association in Kandy, Sri Lanka, in discussion with the author. December. Transcript available upon request.

18 Interview Participant 4. 2018. Anonymous tea farmer, Cooperative Association in Kandy, Sri Lanka, in discussion with the author. December. Transcript available upon request.

19 Interview Participant 8. 2018. Anonymous tea farmer, Cooperative Association in Kandy, Sri Lanka, in discussion with the author. December. Transcript available upon request.

20 Interview Participant 16. 2017. Anonymous coffee farmer, Cooperative Association in Huehuetenango, Guatemala, in discussion with the author. March. Transcript available upon request.

21 Interview Participant 3. 2018. Anonymous tea farmer, Cooperative Association in Kandy, Sri Lanka, in discussion with the author. December. Transcript available upon request.

22 Interview Participant 14. 2018. Anonymous tea farmer, Cooperative Association in Kandy, Sri Lanka, in discussion with the author. December. Transcript available upon request.

23 Interview Participant 1. 2018. Anonymous tea farmer, Cooperative Association in Kandy, Sri Lanka, in discussion with the author. December. Transcript available upon request.

24 Interview Participant 8. 2018. Anonymous tea farmer, Cooperative Association in Kandy, Sri Lanka, in discussion with the author. December. Transcript available upon request.

25 Interview Participant 9. 2017. Anonymous coffee farmer, Cooperative Association in Huehuetenango, Guatemala, in discussion with the author. March. Transcript available upon request.

26 Tiziano Gomiero, Maurizio Paoletti, and David Pimental, "Energy and environmental issues in organic and conventional agriculture," *Critical Reviews in Plant Sciences*, 27(4) (2008): 239–254. Doi: 10.1080/07352680802225456

27 Hans-Peter Hutter, Abdul Wali Khan, Kathrin Lemmerer, Peter Wallner, Michael Kundi, and Hanns Moshammer, "Cytotoxic and genotoxic effects of pesticide exposure in Male coffee farmworkers of the Jarabacoa region, Dominican Republic," *International Journal of Environmental Research and Public Health*, 15(8) (2018): 1641.

28 Sylvette Monier-Dilhan and Fabian Berges, "Consumers' motivations driving organic demand: Between self interest and sustainability," *Agricultural and Resource Economics Review,* 453 (2016): 522–538. Doi: 10.1017/age.2016.6

Part III
The Industries Evolve

7 Democratizing Coffee and Tea Value Chains from the Field to the Cup

Introduction

The oldest continuously operating green coffee importer in the United States is based in New Orleans, housed in an alleyway in the French Quarter. When I was a PhD student at Tulane, I visited their offices. A good friend was working there and offered to bring me in for a tour and a coffee cupping. He knew I had become steeped in the industry through my dissertation research, and this was a rare opportunity to be exposed to one of the first coffee importers in the United States, having opened in New Orleans in 1851. I rode my scooter to the French Quarter, where parking and public transit were sparse, and knocked on an unassuming door down an alley just north of Canal Street.

I entered an aromatic wood-paneled room that was filled with coffee and tea paraphernalia, burlap sacks, and antique furniture. We sat down at a large round wooden table that had been set up for a cupping, or coffee tasting. I had only recently learned how to properly "cup" when I was visiting a large coffee roaster and exporter outside of Antigua in Guatemala. For the uninitiated coffee, cupping involves a combination of visual observation of the color, olfactory appreciation of the brew, and then the spooning and slurping of the warm liquid across the tongue to spread and aerate the flavors. Similar to the more well-known wine tasting process, the cupping of coffee and tasting of tea involves a ritual of appreciation, observation, tasting, and categorizing of scents and flavors. The coffee wheel, established in 1995 by the Specialty Coffee Association and revised since, had developed attributes and a vocabulary to describe the delicate nuances of coffees in all their splendor.[1]

After I had properly embarrassed myself by demonstrating my neophyte cupping technique, a few staff sat down with us to share. Through our conversation, I learned more from their perspective about the

DOI: 10.4324/9781003228851-11

evolution of their work in the coffee industry. I learned how they have shifted their business operations along the way, from colonial origins to this new, more democratized global market. Up to that point, I had been immersed in learning from farmers about the growing process, their livelihoods, and their perspectives on sustainability. But stepping into this office was a reminder of the original structures of the coffee and tea industries, which emerged out of colonialism. While the residue of history remains, as the coffee and tea industries have evolved, some of these markets have begun to decolonize to a certain extent. The colonial plantation model which once relied on slave labor and indentured servitude has shifted to privatized farms with seasonal wage workers.

In some instances, like in Sri Lanka, the land has been redistributed to smallholder farmers who have become cooperative members. The rise of fair trade and the accompanying support for smallholder agriculture and cooperative organizations is evidence of this evolution of values in the global market. Even with the rise of the fair trade system, cash-crop agriculture still favors those further up the supply chain: those with land, those with power and influence as traders, and exporters and importers. Yet at the same time, the economics of coffee and tea have evolved, in part thanks to sustainable business certifications like fair trade, and the movement of these industries toward more sustainable models that consider all three spheres of sustainability: the social, the environmental, and the economic.

My journey began with the farmers, understanding their perspectives, values, and experiences. It ended in the roasteries, at the tasting table, in the cafes, and standing in front of the vast shelves of coffee and tea sold by modern retailers. From my time in Guatemala and in Sri Lanka, what I had distilled at a very basic level was that institutional support of the cooperatives and their respective federations was critical for farmer successes in both a local and global context. At the local level, individual farmers were able to access more profitable returns on their harvest, gain access to training and technical assistance, resources, and leadership opportunities. Through the conduit of these institutions, farmers were able to access the global support of specialty coffee and tea. This opportunity structure expands beyond the boundaries of the cooperative, the federation, and the government. The next chapter explores the perspectives on sustainability from supply chain actors connected to the coffee and tea organizations from the preceding case studies.

Industry Observations

While the formal interviews conducted with these supply chain actors are at the center of this chapter, I also had the opportunity to observe a variety of coffee and tea supply chain professionals at several large industry expos. The observations from these events have helped give shape and form to the perspectives and stories shared in discussion. In August of 2017, I attended the International Specialty Coffee Expo that was held in Puebla, Mexico. I attended as a volunteer and I was given the role of helping English language attendees with issues and questions. The expo was held in a huge convention center up on a hill in Puebla, overlooking the Spanish colonial city center. The expo hall was gigantic and housed a variety of different sections. To the far right were all the value-added coffee adjacent foods, drinks, and accessories. I snapped up free samples of my favorite "natural" gum and purchased some "healthy" obleas, paper-thin large wafer deserts made with millet flour and sweetened with a layer of creamy hazelnut chocolate. In the center of the entrance to the expo was the International Women's Coffee Alliance set up with all the flags from their member countries, and a variety of big coffee lounge areas: Nescafé, Starbucks, Illy.

As I ventured further into the expo, I came across an amazing variety of small roasters from across Latin America. Also present, a significant number of cooperatives and producers sharing stories, pouring samples, and discussing this year's harvest. I was able to attend several of the technical assistance workshops, and there was an entire lecture series around sustainability and organic coffee. For the fortunate folks who were representing their cooperatives, this was the opportunity to meet and interact with peers from around the hemisphere. They could learn first-hand about the most cutting-edge approaches to growing, processing, roasting, packaging, and branding.

Curious to dig deeper into the world of specialty coffee, I attended the Specialty Coffee Association Expo in Seattle in 2018. It was the 30 year anniversary of the event, held at the convention center in downtown. Trying to stretch my meager PhD funding, I stayed at the Buddhist Monastery in the International District, which was hosting guests via Airbnb. I also served as a volunteer to gain entrance into the otherwise costly event. This time I was assisting star Baristas at one of the coffee stations. My service industry skills came in handy from my time in college and graduate school working in restaurants, and through participant observation I learned depths about how baristas engage in customer-facing education and awareness raising, all the while crafting the perfect latte. The energy at the SCA Expo was incredibly high – maybe it was all of the caffeine? Everywhere you looked and listened, there was intentional industry-wide messaging around sustainability. "Coffee is Not Just Coffee," a documentary film and brand seemed to be everywhere with posters, discussions, and tables. Emblematic of the supply chain and customer-facing ethics around elevating coffee as a mechanism for change, this idea would continue to resurface in my formal interviews with coffee and tea professionals throughout my research.

While I never put aside my fascination with the coffee industry, as I became immersed in the world of tea through my work in Sri Lanka, I was curious to see what the industry-level equivalent event was like in the Tea Industry. In 2019, the World Tea Expo was held at a glitzy hotel and conference space in downtown Las Vegas in the summer. Not my venue or season of choice, but it was fairly close to my new outpost in the Sonoran Desert as a professor at the University of Arizona in the McGuire Center for Entrepreneurship. I wandered around the trade floor, talking with various tea retailers and tea industry folks. Mesmerized, I passed through the aisles of automatic tea bagging machines, the rows upon rows of loose leaf tea, and the quaint tea tasting tables set up by traditional Chinese tea sellers. The full spectrum of the specialty tea industry was on display, from the very traditional loose leaf to the scented and blended varieties, to the more experimental single-serving tea beverages like Bubble tea, Kombucha, and even a new tea soda. In my conversations, I consistently heard people from the industry using specialty coffee as a measuring stick or point of comparison for how far tea has come and where the opportunities lie for the future.

There was definitely an overall sentiment about the incredible opportunity that the tea market has for expansion, especially with the rise in popularity of single-serving beverages in the tea category. Neophyte tea entrepreneurs lurked around trade booths and in the workshops, asking enthusiastically about fair trade, and how to communicate the health benefits of tea to different customer segments. However, at the same time that there was a clear revival happening within the industry, it was clear that there was both a reverence for the history and culture of tea, and at the same time residual stagnancy. It reminded me of the layer of tea leaves that settle at the bottom of a hot cup of tea or the sludgy layer that coats the bottom of a bottle of kombucha.

Supply Chain Perspectives

Over the course of the five years that I spent trying to better understand the industry side of the coffee and tea worlds I attended events, visited workshops, imbibed at cafes and retailers, and obsessed over coffee and tea packaging. This provided a rich backdrop for the formal interviews that I conducted, which were more focused on understanding the specific dynamics of the supply chains connected to the cooperatives in Guatemala and Sri Lanka. Not surprisingly, most of the people I spoke with in the coffee and tea industries were incredibly passionate and opinionated about their work, and enthusiastically shared their perspectives on trends happening both locally and globally.

There was a deep recognition of the history of these industries, and the lack of sustainability integrated into their original architecture. And yet, there was an incredible amount of hope around the opportunities that currently exist to create more sustainable structures, from economic reform to environmental responsibility and social justice. Above all, there was an overall sentiment around the importance of the relational and collaborative aspects of their business operations across the supply chain, which echoed themes from research on collective impact. In the fields of business ethics and social entrepreneurship, this area of the study argues that collaboration with different stakeholders contributes to accessing the innovative potential that exists within the cooperative relationship while increasing the value and quality of processes and outputs.[2,3] Perhaps most importantly, it has been argued that the collective impact approach is essential for dismantling outdated institutional arrangements and creating more sustainable systems.[4]

Most coffee and tea professionals that I spoke with were hyper-aware of the dark colonial past of both industries, and the changes that have happened over time. In the coffee industry, one exporter from Guatemala shared more about the massive shift that has happened at the production level as a result of the global coffee crash during the 1990s:

There has been a big shift in the coffee industry in the last decade or two. When there was the big coffee crash in the 1990s, the majority of the large finca (farm) owners opted out of coffee because it wasn't worth it to them anymore. It cost too much to pay workers to harvest the coffee by hand, which is necessary, and they weren't able to sell their coffee for enough. As you may know, in the lower altitudes only the Robusta coffee grows. Anyhow, this shifted to the coffee industry in the hands almost completely of small producers. Now, coffee represents the one way that it is still possible to make a livelihood as a small producer, living in the mountains. This is partly because of the fact that the Arabica coffee thrives only at high altitudes, and that is where the small farmers are based. The big finca (farm) owners, they didn't want to live up there, to move their production.[5]

In contrast, most supply chain actors that I spoke with in the tea industry commented on how slow the industry has been to change. In comparison to the specialty coffee industry, where the cooperative movement in combination with sustainable business certifications have created more widespread changes, in tea this has been a challenge. One retailer shared:

The tea industry is just so government influenced, it is founded on very antiquated practices, and the tea boards in each country require a certain percentage gets sold through the tea auction. Even if you are direct sale. Most gardens, that is not an issue, because that is what they do. They are large plantations that grow thousands of acres, hundreds of thousands of acres to sell at auction, full stop. And that is the business.[6]

Everyone had opinions on the role of farmers, and how the supply chain works to support them. This is partly out of the shared motivation to reform the industry and to enhance sustainability through collaborative relationships. It also comes out of their own business goals to roast, supply, and serve the best specialty coffee possible. When I spoke with coffee industry representatives and those working closely with farmers, many shared this sentiment. One manager of the coffee federation reflected:

The most important part of supporting small producers is supporting their decisions. Giving them the power and the opportunity to make decisions and be in charge. The old way of doing things was that post-colonial buyers would come in, sample the coffee, and then go to the producers, "ok, I will take this many bags from you, and this many bags from you, and I will pay this much." Now, it is better with the cooperative structure, not ideal of course, but better. At least the cooperatives are at the bargaining table. And with the fair trade premiums, cooperatives choose how the premiums will be spent. So instead of projects being dictated to them, they decide what is most important to the community. Whether it is education, or a health project, or a project to strengthen the capacity of the cooperative's operations. This is why having farmers in decision-making positions is important.[7]

While the tea industry at large has predominantly maintained the plantation style of agriculture, in the case of Sri Lanka, MOPA and Bio Foods were somewhat of an exception. One of the federation managers shared proudly their perspective as an outlier in the industry:

> At the tea federation we always help the farmers develop and increase their living standards. It is easier for us to work with farmers. It used to be the case that their standard of living was very low, because people never took care of the plantation workers. It was a precedent that was set when the British introduced the system. Cash crop agriculture, whatever the commodity. What we do, is we provide them with the fairtrade premium and that is preferrable from both ends. At the moment we are working with farming communities.[8]

The founder of Bio Foods shared his perspective about the important interconnections that exist between farmers, economic sustainability, and the environment:

> When we started, we had other challenges. Without human beings, you cannot look after the soil, so first we had to look after the human beings, with economic development. So that is how I started in 1993, I started this project then. At that time, fair trade was not yet a thing. Actually, I was one of the primary people helping to set standards. We have to respect the basic human needs: how can you ensure income? Why do people join companies in the private sector to earn a salary? Because you have income assurance – it is a great assurance. People don't worry about the amount as much; they worry more about the assurance so that they can plan their life. But in the typical agriculture system, farmers don't have either: assurance about a steady salary or knowing the amount. We have to change this system. The basic tenants that will never really change is the relationship with the farmers. I realized really quickly; you get things done based on personal relationships. Nothing is really even written down based on contracts. They have to like you. If they don't like you, nothing is happening. I don't know how efficient that is, but that is how it functions. Plus, you know, its basic human relationships. You can't forget that this is people growing this with their own hands. Regardless of the market price, we always give the fair trade price plus all of the fair trade premiums. And we are trying to maintain organic because the UK has been projecting that in 40 years there

won't be any healthy soil left because of the fertilizer and chemicals used. We are trying to build a land bank that still has soil microbes left.[9]

These ideas about sustainable livelihoods in agriculture have long been studied, demonstrating exactly this conclusion.[10] In order for agriculture to be environmentally sustainable, the practices and protocols must align with human culture and sustenance. Further along the supply chain in the coffee and tea industry, representatives echoed this sentiment. In the coffee industry, one of the early adopters of organic coffee purchasing, roasting, and retail shared his perspective:

I like to buy certified organic, but I don't think it's enough on its own. They also have to be actually doing sustainable practices. It needs to be hand in hand. The organic has to do with avoiding chemicals in my mind. There is almost no way that if you are using chemicals that it is not going to leach into groundwater, and that whoever is picking the coffee is not going to be exposed or impacted physically. And perhaps generationally, because of the damage that the chemicals do, it will affect their children. Just thinking about that kills my desire to drink coffee. We need to be good custodians of the land. So that is why, and we try to add organic in when we can. The thing is, if you were to think about – a farmer grows a certain amount of coffee, this is his crop. All grown and treated in the same way. He is certified organic, certified fair trade, or she, mostly, and she is certified with some sort of sustainable mark. But these certificates, they cost money. So maybe this grower can only afford to get half certified as organic. Or maybe it's all organic, but only half is fair trade certified. Right, but maybe a quarter of it is Rainforest Alliance (RFA). It's not like on this half they used slaves, and on this half they didn't. Right? Or on this half they did something different. It's all the same coffee, it's just how much they can afford in terms of certification. So, we often will buy from a farm and say, this year we were able to get fair trade, but not next year. We are still going to buy the coffee, because we know the labor practices are in line with fair trade. If we can get the RFA added we do. This is all grown in the same way. So if we feel like even though it does not have the certification, we are supporting a farm that is certified and supporting their efforts.[11]

The certification is an outward signifier of the practices happening at the farm level. However, there are often administrative, logistical, and cost-related barriers that might prevent smallholders from getting organic certification, and the transition process can be challenging.[12] This is where supply chain stakeholders who believe in the organic movement come in to support the development of a larger organic market. One of the federation managers went on to support this experience from the tea industry as well. He shared the process of how farmers become associated with the organization and how they benefit from the administration, consolidation, and resources:

> The farming family will handle their land, and then they are all organized by the organization. We handle the paperwork for the certification and we pay for it and everything. They can't, we do it for them. So, it starts at people's homes on their farms. It is very grassroots.[13]

At the institutional level, the tea federation continued to support these benefits:

> You need to have a system for traceability too, so that you can help the farmers to improve. Now, IFOAM is the main group. That is one of the reasons we started the cooperatives was so that small farmers could become organic certified.[14]

Here, we can observe the coordination that takes place at a nested level, with the cooperative and federation structure serving as an organizing force, bringing farmers on board, providing technical and administrative support, and helping to coordinate certification. At the level of the supply chain, buyers that export, import, roast, and sell create the demand and also the support for certified products. In addition to organic certification, supply chain stakeholders also shared their perspectives on fair trade. One buyer who supports the system shared:

> Fair trade is just a phenomenal concept, and is responsible for not just consumer level, but industry awareness of the issues of the people who are growing our products for us. I think fair trade sort of brought some of that awareness to the world. There are different flavors of fair trade now, there is Fairtrade International and Fairtrade USA. We are with Fairtrade USA because I like their more inclusive philosophy, because it does not restrict the fair trade price to the cooperative setting. So individual farmers can get a fair trade price as well if they are meeting the components of the program, which really is what, I think, it's about. Its about

increasing the life quality of the people involved in the food chain, so I don't really like the exclusionary thing because I think it can be abused, and I think Fairtrade International is trying to address that.[15]

At the same time, this buyer discussed the challenge of buying fair trade and/or organic certified coffee from a supply perspective.

Again, sometimes they ask for fair trade and we can't get it. That is why we are trying to do more direct trade. We make a deal with the farmer and we hire an importer and they handle the transactions, because I am not an importer, and nor do I want to be one. We are trying to create our own framework, like "impact coffee," so we have a positive impact on this person, even though they are not certified. Maybe we pay a premium towards their fair trade projects. So even though it isn't certified – this is something I started thinking about yesterday. Gee, if they aren't certified, why wouldn't we do something to help them put money towards their fair trade project? Even though their lot of coffee may not actually be certified. I like the idea. For me, it's more about rewarding the choices that farmers make.[16]

A tea retailer echoed these sentiments, while also highlighting the comparatively sluggish progress in the tea industry toward improving conditions for tea workers:

For the estate owners, I mean humane and fair treatment of these folks who are making the product possible is key. There is plenty of room for improvement there. Tea is a wildly profitable product. At every step of the way, past the pluckers, it is really juicy, juicy margins. And can some of that be trickled back down? Probably. But the whole industry is built on very cheap labor, and we are just a little speck, but the whole industry is based on it. Some of it is going to mechanization, which has its pros and cons, but yea, it is an ancient very top heavy influenced supply chain. We really wish we had demand for more quality product, because overall, tea is still very much a commodity product. IT is just so big. You do have to make changes, mostly worker focused practices, and that is just the nature of fair trade. It is worker focused, and I think organics gives consumers comfort on the agricultural practices, and so fairtrade on the labor practices.[17]

The entire supply chain is dependent on consumers demand, and consumer awareness and education are an integral part of this support. A common theme that arose in both industries was around storytelling and educating consumers. One coffee retailer shared:

> When we had a week ago, for world Fair Trade Day, a celebration, many of our vendors were there, and people could see the variety of products. And people telling the story about where the products are from, and here is what I am seeing on the ground. Bit by bit, that education happens. Obviously, if someone is really committed to fair trade, they will seek that out. Is it a little more expensive - sometimes it is, sometimes it isn't, but ok. I always say, we have a really serious immigration issue that is really costing us a lot of money, to say nothing about people's lives. Oh, why is that, well, because they can't afford to stay home. Try to help people connect the dots. So, pay now, pay later. Now, if you have absolutely no money, that's a different deal. We are talking about people who can afford to make choices.[18]

Although consumer awareness in the coffee industry is arguably higher, in tea there is still a lot of work to be done. One retailer commented:

> The consumer awareness of tea is nowhere, nowhere. People don't realize tea is a plant, it is insane, how little people know about this industry. So, consumers just don't care. You have your group of tea geeks, as we call them, and they get it, but even there, it is just the knowledge of what this industry looks like, how its cultivated, and that you know, real women with families and lives are picking their tea every day. No one knows, no one has looked. People drink iced tea, and they don't even realize its tea. So, there is just this chasm of awareness and consciousness in this industry and why, I don't know. Even in England, a high tea consuming country. They don't know. They think they are experts, but there is just utter consumer ignorance. It is just there is no knowledge, much less demand for knowledge. Coffee, and wine, those industries are much further along. And you know in coffee, there is a heavy commodification of coffee, but a decent chunk of it has managed to get a little richer. It is bizarre. This industry is just weird, such a long way to go.[19]

Echoing this sentiment, a coffee retailer shared:

> From an education perspective, certification is the most impactful and powerful. Social justice is really hard, and usually you don't feel like you are making any impact. This [fair trade] makes it really easy. I can, by the thing I choose to buy, make a difference, help people educate their kids in their village, live a better life, it was just this big light bulb, that this makes sense.[20]

And this sentiment around the importance of certification, education, and awareness raising as a positive feedback cycle was also observed by a tea industry representative:

> Once consumers learn about the importance of organic and what the difference is with conventional farming practices, it is pretty straight forward. People drink tea for many reasons, a large one is health. The tea plant is very healthy for you, but when you learn it is coated in pesticides, it kind of negates the health benefits of it... and then there are a lot of consumers that are just really committed to organic, on every agricultural level. So, you know, some folks who are just committed and believe in the value of chemical free food. We have had customers write to us and tell us that they have tasted the chemicals in conventional teas, and that this is why they have moved over to organic. They would rather drink tea, than chemicals. So, lots of reasons.[21]

In addition to sharing their perspectives on the importance of certifications at various levels of the supply chain, and one tea industry representative very aptly summarized why they thought consumers were drawn to products with certified labels:

> I think that people like labels because it makes them feel safe. They don't have to think too much about what is behind all of this. The transactions from the ground up can be verified. Most consumers just want to buy something and feel good about it. The certifications serve to make people feel better about what they are buying. But most people don't even really know what they mean. For now, certifications are what we have, but education is most important. At least people are motivated and prefer this. It is better than what we were doing before – we are all about labels anyways. With the heart of the people, who buy the products: you

don't need to go against corporations, just education and prove to the people that this style of agriculture can give a better product.[22]

As they reflected on their roles in the value chain and speculated on consumer habits from their observations, several themes emerged about the future of the industry. This included the power that they wield as support structures for creating more sustainability in the coffee and tea industries. One buyer commented on how their success and growth yields more impact at the farm level and for farming families. He shared:

> So, you get to a certain size, and you find that you can do more things, you can buy larger quantities and have a bigger impact - you know, you are throwing a stone into a pond, but now it's an even bigger stone, so the ripple is bigger and you can impact more people positively. That is where we are at. We are trying to do stuff like that right now.[23]

Another retailer shared their perspective. This is a growing perspective in the business world that claims business is not only about economic gain, but also about creating justice and translating your values through your business practices. They relayed:

> We have to understand that everything is not about money, and we need to look at happiness. How happy can you be? From companies to producers themselves, knowing that this is a game of life, and whatever you give will come back to you, and has more to do with values and with our own humanity. Its more than just the supply chain. Once we are more aware of fairness, there is more sustainability. Companies are making much more profit than the farmers, but then I see the farmers exploiting their workers. If we have more awareness of our values and fairness then we can invest in people and their own potential. Farmers need to reclaim their dignity and be aware that they can keep dreaming and achieve and be awakened. In both sides there is the need to be aware of going beyond their comfort zones/trajectory as money makers or victims. To be aware – this is the basis of change.[24]

Tea industry representatives were also cautiously optimistic and saw the possibility of emulating the windfall of change that has been sweeping the specialty coffee industry. One importer shared:

Tea is an industry with so much potential, it's an industry surrounded by other industries that really have made seismic shifts, and it feels like tea is going to. I think it's also that tea is only part of it for me. It's as much a vehicle for everything we stand for. For clean food, for ethical practices, for education. I see our product as a tool for education on the food system. So yeah, it's definitely, there is definitely bigger picture stuff in there for me. Tea is just a funny category – how do we start to get this industry out of the colonial period? The challenge is just magnificent, and I think the potential impact that this industry can exert from origin to consumer is huge.[25]

The opportunities that exist are abundant. Supply chain stakeholders were not naive in their understanding of the challenges that exist and the enormous change that is possible with coordinated efforts. Efforts that center around actionable and measurable tools. Another tea industry professional observed the critical role of the supply chain in creating this change:

The supply chain is everything. The workers I mean, the gap between worker wages and what happens over here is just mind blowing. The worker empowerment, it is almost even nonexistent in this industry. So the opportunities are many: unless your whole supply chain is sustainable and everyone along the chain is satisfied, you cannot really run this type of business sustainability.[26]

In the case of the specialty tea and coffee supply chains, there have been waves of changes as a result of the coordination between farmers, agricultural institutions. This ties back into the key role of collaboration and collective impact within both the coffee and tea industries. The creation of networks and the development of new synergies are essential for improving the sustainability of operations.[27] This type of collaboration within supply chains is crucial, as indicated via the insightful observations of these coffee and tea professionals. The collective impact approach demands that systemic change requires broad-based coordination and cross-sector commitment to a common agenda.[28]

Conclusion

The overall purpose of this chapter has been to understand the perspectives of global supply chain actors whose purchasing power and influence at the level of the international coffee supply chain directly impacts the institutions that support coffee producers at origin. To achieve this purpose, the perspectives of supply chain stakeholders have been explored regarding the role of small farmers and their supply chains in creating more sustainable models in the coffee and tea industries. These findings have highlighted ways in which actors and institutions further along the supply chain contribute to the process of change within agricultural institutions and industries.

This process is inextricably influenced by the values and priorities of exporters, importers, retailers, and technical assistance organizations connected to the coffee industry, even extending to the perceived preferences and values of consumers. Various supply chain actors realistically reflected on the reality of the slow evolution of sustainability in the coffee and tea industries. Their perspectives and experiences about best practices for enhancing sustainability through grassroots level observations are important insights that contribute to a better understanding of the role that institutions linked at multiple levels can play in enhancing sustainability across the supply chain. Just as the collective impact has served as a powerful force amongst coffee and tea farmers in their cooperatives and federations, so too does this extend to the macro level with the supply chain.

This practical understanding of the importance of considering how the context "at origin" can inform the success of programs and policies aimed at supporting sustainability. This goes beyond superficial greening strategies. By tailoring sustainability strategies to the local context, resources can be more effectively targeted to further enhance this process of change. For example, buyers working with farmers and their cooperatives as they transition to organic agriculture may be critical, while simultaneously channeling resources into educational trainings. The organizational settings at the producer level, nested within the levels of the global supply chain present a particularly powerful setting for change, where sustainability practices can be reinforced not only in theory but also in practice. This type of approach may lead to wider scale integration of sustainability practices. Perhaps most importantly, it has the potential to result in the genuine transformation of the coffee and tea industries.

Notes

1 "Coffee Flavor Wheel," Specialty Coffee Association (1995), Accessed online: http://www.scaa.org/?d=scaaflavorwheel&page=resources
2 Antonio Tencati and Laszlo Zsolnai, "The collaborative enterprise," *Journal of Business Ethics,* 85(3) (2009): 367–376. https://doi.org/10.1007/s10551-008-9775-3
3 Gerry Gereffi and Joonkoo Lee, "Economic and social upgrading in global value chains and industrial clusters: Why governance matters," *Journal of Business Ethics*, 133(1) (2016): 25–38. https://doi.org/10.1007/s10551014-2373

4 Franziska Kullak, Julia Fehrer, Jonathan Baker, Herbert Woratschek, and Joanna Sam-Cobbah, "Shaping market systems for social change in emerging economies," *Industrial Marketing Management*, 100 (2022): 19–35. https://doi.org/10.1016/j.indmarman.2021.10.014

5 Interview Participant 18. 2017. Anonymous coffee exporter, Antigua, Guatemala, in discussion with the author. April. Transcript available upon request.

6 Interview Participant 3. 2019. Anonymous tea retailer, Video Interview, in discussion with the author. July. Transcript available upon request.

7 Interview Participant 12. 2017. Anonymous coffee federation manager, Quetzaltenango, Guatemala, in discussion with the author. March. Transcript available upon request.

8 Interview Participant 2. 2018. Anonymous tea federation manager, Kandy, Sri Lanka, in discussion with the author. December. Transcript available upon request.

9 Interview Participant 1. 2017. Tea federation founder, Kandy Sri Lanka, in discussion with the author. November. Transcript available upon request.

10 Ian Scoones, "Sustainable rural livelihoods: A framework for analysis," *IDS Working Paper*, 72 (1998) Brighton: IDS.

11 Interview Participant 8. 2017. Anonymous coffee retailer, Video Interview, in discussion with the author. June. Transcript available upon request.

12 Laura Reynolds, "The globalization of organic agro-food networks," *World Development*, 32(5) (2004): 725–743. https://doi.org/10.1016/j.worlddev.2003.11.008

13 Interview Participant 2. 2018. Anonymous tea federation manager, Kandy, Sri Lanka, in discussion with the author. December. Transcript available upon request.

14 Interview Participant 1. 2017. Tea federation founder, Kandy, Sri Lanka, in discussion with the author. November. Transcript available upon request.

15 Interview Participant 22. 2018. Anonymous tea buyer, Video Interview, in discussion with the author. December. Transcript available upon request.

16 Interview Participant 9. 2017. Anonymous coffee roaster, Video Interview, in discussion with the author. June. Transcript available upon request.

17 Interview Participant 3. 2019. Anonymous tea retailer, Video Interview, in discussion with the author. July. Transcript available upon request.

18 Interview Participant 13. 2017. Anonymous coffee retailer, Video Interview, in discussion with the author. June. Transcript available upon request.

19 Interview Participant 3. 2019. Anonymous tea retailer, Video Interview, in discussion with the author. July. Transcript available upon request.

20 Interview Participant 13. 2017. Anonymous coffee retailer, Video Interview, in discussion with the author. June. Transcript available upon request.

21 Interview Participant 5. 2019. Anonymous tea retailer, Video Interview, in discussion with the author. July. Transcript available upon request.

22 Interview Participant 2. 2017. Anonymous tea federation staff, Kandy, Sri Lanka, in discussion with the author. November. Transcript available upon request.

23 Interview Participant 8. 2017. Anonymous coffee retailer, Video Interview, in discussion with the author. June. Transcript available upon request.

24 Interview Participant 14. 2017. Anonymous coffee retailer, Video Interview, in discussion with the author. June. Transcript available upon request.
25 Interview Participant 7. 2019. Anonymous tea retailer, Video Interview, in discussion with the author. July. Transcript available upon request
26 Interview Participant 10. 2019. Anonymous tea retailer, Video Interview, in discussion with the author. July. Transcript available upon request
27 Alessandra De Chiara, "Collective impact approach: A 'tool' for managing complex problems and business clusters sustainability," *Metropolitan Universities,* 28(4) (2017): 101–114.
28 J. Kania and M. Kramer, "Collective impact," Stanford Social Innovation Review, Winter 2011. http://ssir.org/articles/entry/collective_impact

8 Riding the Waves: A Sustainable Future for Coffee and Tea

Introduction

By the end of my research in Sri Lanka, the federation had moved from a smaller headquarters in Kandy to a large modern building at the edge of Colombo, on the Kandy to Colombo highway. There was better access to the port for importing and exporting, and they were closer to the domestic market concentrated in the capital. They had expanded their business to include not just organic fair trade teas, but also a range of spices. There was even a growing operation of organic turmeric in Myanmar that was then imported and packed for distribution internationally through the federation.

On my last day in Sri Lanka, I made my way from Kandy to the new headquarters for some final conversations, as well as to check out their new organic shop. Through my discussions with the federation leadership, I had come to learn that while tea was an important cornerstone of the business, a main goal for the company has been to establish a domestic market for organics. As a start to this process, they had recently launched a market on the first floor of their headquarters as a demonstration project. The market was incredibly stylish, decorated in an upscale farmhouse décor with floating wood shelves filled with organic teas, spices, treacle, and grains. Accompanying this was a large farmhouse table in the center featuring bins of local organic vegetables.

As I spoke with one of the staff, it became clear that this shop was the manifestation of decades of work. This work included establishing the cooperatives, creating a foundational export business, and was now moving toward establishing a thriving local market for organics. They had catalyzed a sustainable model for not just the production of tea, but for local agriculture more broadly. Due to their innovative work, planting the seeds for the organic movement in Sri Lanka, representatives from Bio Foods now serve on the country's panel to support the country-wide

DOI: 10.4324/9781003228851-12

conversion to organics. This process takes time: not just years, but decades. With the proper institutional support, systems can shift.

In Guatemala, prospects for scaling and expansion were also on the horizon. During my last visit to the cooperative, they shared with me a jar of honey from their coffee pollination project that they had prepared as part of their diversification efforts. The federation had already started expanding their product lines to feature organic herbal teas like lemongrass and hibiscus, coffee honey, cacao beans, and organic granulized panela (a less processed sugar product).

As I have followed their progress from afar, it has been inspiring to watch projects that were just a dream turn into reality. When I had attended the annual federation meeting that brought together representatives from all the cooperatives, there had been discussion of long-term diversification into agrotourism and expansion of their products and in-country cafes. On the main page of their website, they now have information about an ecotourism project where visitors can explore a nature preserve, stay in green-built accommodations, and learn about the coffee production process through visits with local coffee producers connected to the federation. All these linked efforts create enhanced sustainability for the producers and the federation by increasing livelihood diversification and expanding business opportunities, all while protecting the natural environment through conservation, agroecology, and education.

What elements are necessary to ensure a sustainable future in the coffee and tea industries moving forward? This book has shared the case of two exemplary models: one in coffee and one in tea. Both point to several key lessons to be learned for sustainability in not just coffee and tea, but across agriculture and beyond.

Lesson One: Institutional Support

One of the main lessons is in the power of institutions. From the cooperative structure to the federation, these organizational forms have provided critical support for sustainability. At the economic and social levels, these institutions support not only farmers but also the supply chain. For farmers, the cooperative provides access to resources that increase their autonomy, agency, empowerment, and well-being. Through their cooperatives and respective federations, farmers earn more for their crops and have opportunities for diversification.

Institutional support also provides increased access to buyers willing to pay a higher price. For actors further up the value chain, the cooperatives and federations provide mechanisms for not only purchasing high-quality coffee and tea but for ensuring transparency of process and pricing. At the social level, farmers gain important benefits through these organizations from technical assistance to peer exchange and learning. At the individual level, they gain confidence, skills, and agency. Through the democratically run institutions, members have the opportunity to participate in decision-making, and vote on projects and key strategies. This supports collective empowerment. In terms of environmental sustainability, not only do the cooperatives provide technical assistance for converting to organic, but they ensure ongoing support as farmers continue to confront a variety of issues from monkeys and wild boars to La Roya and dwindling water supplies.

Lesson Two: Certifications

Another main lesson concerns the role of sustainable business certifications. While certainly not a panacea, in both cases fair trade and organic certifications have served as vehicles for catalyzing sustainability. In terms of economic sustainability, certifications like fair trade and organic have garnered higher prices throughout the supply chain. Farmers receive more for certified products than conventional uncertified products, and these benefits also accrue across the supply chain. In addition, in the case of fair trade, the annual social premium has also infused capital back into the cooperatives, where they can democratically choose how to invest their funds.

The social premiums are one example of a certification tool that contributes to not just economic sustainability but social sustainability as well. Through the social premiums, farmers have chosen not only to reinvest back into their businesses, but also into their communities through education funds, school garden programs, and other community development projects. As a result of fair trade standards, inclusivity and equity are also interwoven into the membership and functioning of the cooperatives. Through the education and training initiatives of the cooperative, fair trade principles related to gender equity can be offered and embedded into the organizational structures. Finally, certifications like fair trade and organic offer transparent standards. With the help of institutional structures such as the cooperative and the federation, the common barriers to achieving certification are easier to overcome.

Lesson Three: Supply Chain Support

The final lesson that emerged from these two cases, to quote one of the research participants, is that the supply chain is everything. The impact of these actions and activities are amplified through the coordinated efforts and shared values of the businesses collaborating to bring sustainably produced coffee and tea to market. Through this collective work, farmers are helping to create a new model for global commerce that has enabled the further democratization of these once colonial industries.

The Next Waves

What will the next wave look like? Current efforts already underway in coffee, tea, and across other industries point toward the path for sustainability into the future. In the realm of institutional support, there continues to be evidence that demonstrates the central role that democratically run organizations play in supporting farmers. While changes to the fair trade system have bifurcated the market for smallholders, there is potential and opportunity with the rise of direct trade as part of current and future waves in coffee and tea.

In the realm of certification, the rise of direct trade, the regenerative agriculture certification, and the B Lab certification all offer evidence of the continued dedication and progress toward building more sustainable systems through collective impact. These efforts are developing simultaneously but draw on the cumulative efforts of decades of work by farmers, cooperatives, and supply chain actors. Direct trade has emerged out of the third wave specialty movement, which seeks to improve upon the fair trade model by forging more direct relationships between farmers and buyers. Direct trade, though not a formal third-party verified certification, is a label that denotes a high price paid to farmers and frequent visits by roasters and retailers to the farm. A major motivation for creating direct trade was the justification that achieving quality requires knowledge and crafting of a product's entire process, from the farm to the cup. It is distinguished from the fair trade concept through its intentional focus on the importance of the relationship between the farmer and the roaster/buyer.

Although direct trade is not currently an independently audited certification, many specialty roasters and retailers have adopted a shared set of principles. An integral benefit of this type of relationship is that it transforms a transactional relationship to a more interactive and iterative exchange. This echoes many of the sentiments from the supply chain in these case studies, where there was a recognition of the unique opportunity. This allows buyers to not only directly buy from farmers, but to work with them on improving farming practices that support the growth of not only a higher quality product but a more sustainably produced one as well. In addition to creating a price premium guarantee, the purpose is to empower farming communities.[1,2] Since this is a relatively new phenomenon, there is minimal research and evidence that has evaluated this approach. In theory, it demonstrates another major shift in the coffee and tea industries. It moves away from anonymous transactions between producers and buyers, and toward greater transparency while reinforcing mechanisms of values-based relationships within the supply chain.

To address environmental sustainability in agriculture a new certification approach has emerged. This new approach is built on the progress of the organic movement. Organic certification has increased exponentially over the last few decades. Building on its success is the regenerative agriculture movement's Regenerative Organic Certification program, which just wrapped up a pilot program in 2019. Spearheaded by the Rodale Institute, the regenerative movement evolved out of a groundswell in the organic movement to move beyond sustainability. As the impacts of agriculture on anthropogenic climate change have become undeniable, this movement has argued that simply being sustainable is not enough. Rather, there is a need to repair the extensive damage that humans have caused to the planet. The goal of regenerative agriculture is to improve the land by using approaches that regenerate and revitalize the soil and the environment. The primary aim is to increase the level of organic matter in the soil. This leads to multiple positive outcomes: better resilience to extreme weather events, increased efficiency in the soil's water-holding capacity, fewer diseases due to the beneficial soil biota controlling pathogens, and increases in the bioavailability of nutrients that plants, animals, and humans need.[3]

This approach draws from traditional practices from around the world as well as more than a century of applied research and development. Some of its components, such as cover crops and crop rotation, have been part of organic, biodynamic, and other sustainable farming systems for generations. Indigenous cultures made invaluable contributions to many practices currently used in regenerative agriculture.[4] Overall, regenerative agriculture incorporates a mix of best practices that are known to improve soils and agrobiodiversity. These include agroecology, organic farming practices, no-till/low-till, cover crops, crop rotations, holistic grazing, permaculture, composting, mobile animal shelters, pasture cropping, agroforestry, forest farming, ecological agriculture, and others.[5]

As this approach has gained momentum and support, a formal certification program has been introduced. The Regenerative Organic Certification was launched in 2018 by the nonprofit organization the Regenerative Organic Alliance. It was developed through a cooperative effort among a coalition of farmers, ranchers, nonprofit organizations, scientists, and brands led by the Rodale Institute. Its aim is to reach above the basic organic standards and set guidelines for soil health and land management, animal welfare, and farmer and worker fairness. The guiding inspiration of the certification is to "farm like the world depends on it," and in its current form it relies heavily on leveraging and advancing existing standards. Still in its infancy, a pilot was conducted in 2019 with 19 brands producing commodities as diverse as dairy, mangoes, and cereal grains spanning the globe from Nebraska to Nicaragua. Companies including Patagonia, Dr. Bronner's, Nature's Path Organics, Lotus Foods, and Horizon Dairy are just several amongst this diverse group. The framework that emerged from this experience was revised in 2020 and was based on farmer feedback.[6]

Perhaps the most promising new comprehensive certification that leverages all of the certifications around sustainability is the B Lab certification. This certification has been applied across all industries, and at all levels of the supply chain. Companies, organizations, and institutions that undertake the B Lab certification to become B Corps are businesses that meet the highest standards of verified social and environmental performance, public transparency, and accountability to balance profit and purpose. The central ethos of the B Corps movement is "Using Business as a Force for Good."[7]

As opposed to traditional environmental, social, and governance (ESG) B Corps goes beyond to work with certifying companies to make legal change. This is to integrate stakeholder consideration into the structure of their companies. As of the writing of this book, the certification has been achieved by 4,276 companies across 153 industries in 77 different countries.[8] In the food industry, this ranges from specialty chocolate companies such as Tony's Chocoloney, to large food industry giants such as Danone. You may have noticed the certification, a capital B encircled in black outline on a white background. In many ways, this movement and its corresponding certification represent the culmination of efforts in the private sector to integrate a developmental process for increasing sustainability across the supply chain.

The certification program itself relies on a baseline impact assessment (BIA) that determines a baseline score for a company. The assessment covers five areas of the company's social and environmental performance – Governance, Workers, Community, Environment, and Consumers. In addition to measuring and evaluating best practices related to the company's operational performance, the BIA also identifies and evaluates what is called Impact Business Models (IBMs). IBMs identify how a company's core business model may be designed to create positive social and/or environmental impact. As the company works to improve its rating, it may leverage other certification programs as building blocks. Fairtrade, organic, and other industry-specific certifications can be integrated into a company's efforts to work toward being a force for good.[9]

Currently, there are 128 B Corporations that represent the coffee and tea industries. Of this group, 80 are from coffee and 48 are from tea. The vast majority of these companies represent the third and fourth waves. While Starbucks is not yet a certified B Corporation, if it was it would certainly be the largest B Corporation in the coffee sector. Starbucks was founded in Seattle, Washington in 1971. Originally a wholesale coffee roaster, over the decades the company has transitioned from spearheading the second wave of coffee in the United States to being a global icon in the industry. Over the years, its reputation has shifted from revolutionary to mainstream, as it has adopted a brilliantly successful franchise model. It operates on nearly every urban street corner and even adapted to the suburban drive-through lifestyle. Yet given the power of the coffee industry and how transformative trends can become, even Starbucks has continued to evolve its standards of sustainability alongside the ethics of the subsequent and now emerging waves.

As a company, Starbucks buys approximately 3% of the world's coffee, sourced from 400,00 farmers in 30 countries. Their website acknowledges their understanding of their own scale and impact on the future of coffee farmers and their families. As a leader and behemoth in sustainability, Starbucks is one of the largest purchasers of Fairtrade-certified coffee in the world. In 2003, they created their own set of ethical sourcing standards specific to the coffee industry called CAFÉ (Coffee and Farmer Equity Practices). Developed in collaboration with Conservation International, the program consists of 200 indicators including financial reporting, protecting workers' rights, water conservation, and biodiversity.[10,11]

When I first moved to Seattle, I couldn't help but notice the obtrusively large Starbucks logo at the top of a well-preserved brick factory building in the SODO (South of Downtown) neighborhood, the traditional warehouse district. This was the Starbucks headquarters. I felt a certain sense of awe as I crossed the sidewalk and entered the building. A gleaming Starbucks Reserve coffee shop was set up on the ground floor in partnership with a high-end Italian café serving Neapolitan-style pizza, sandwiches, and salads. It felt more like a museum than a coffee shop, given its size and impressive displays. To the right was an entire oversized coffee bar with almost every coffee brewing contraption known to human society. The French press, the Chemex, the syphon, just to name a few. Of course, you could still order the daily drip brew, pressed out of heated thermos containers in the back. However, should you want a micro lot pour-over this was also the place. Along the entire left side of the café was a wall of coffee bag art commemorating reserve coffees served by the company from countries such as Ethiopia, Panama, and Guatemala. You could opt for a coffee flight, and sample multiple coffees side-by-side, as you would a wine or champagne tasting. The origin flight featured coffee from Rwanda, Bolivia, Colombia, and a whiskey barrel-aged coffee from Guatemala. The brew comparison flight allowed you to try the same coffee, brewed with several different techniques. As one of the main trailblazers of second-wave coffee and the original leader of sustainability in the coffee industry, Starbucks has continued to ride the waves of change and adapt and adopt emerging sustainability practices.

The spectrum of participation in sustainability initiatives at all levels of these industries, from the farmers to the cup demonstrates the power of collaboration. As the waves roll, they say a rising tide raises all ships. From the farmers to the exporters, importers, and retailers. Whether they are direct trade micro-roasteries and coffee houses, or the corner Starbucks.

Achieving sustainability in the coffee and tea industries has become the focus of wide-scale efforts across supply chains. Clearly, it is not defined by a linear process. Perhaps the metaphor of the wave can be extended to also describe the process of pursuing sustainability. To human observation, it appears as though waves are a circular action, moving back and forth towards the coast. Over time, even the course of a day, the movement of a wave has a constant cycle that rolls along the coast. Through the course of years and decades, the movement of waves creates a massive impact upon shorelines over time. Maybe it is the same with sustainability efforts in the coffee and tea industries. Through continuous coordinated effort of farmers, traders, and con-sumers, their activities cumulatively create massive impact over time. It is not a change that happens overnight, but change that happens, *"poco a poco."* And, as I heard many of the farmers in Guatemala say *"vamos a ver"* we will just have to wait and see.

Notes

1 Paul Hindsley, David M. McEvoy, and Ashton Morgan, "Consumer de-mand for ethical products and the role of cultural worldviews: The case of direct-trade coffee," *Ecological Economics,* 177 (2020): 106776.

2 Emil Holland, Chris Kjeldsen, and Søren Kerndrup, "Coordinating quality practices in direct trade coffee," *Journal of Cultural Economy,* 9(2) (2016): 186–196.
3 Andre Leu, "Regenerative agriculture movements," *Organic Food Systems,* (2020): 21.
4 Thomas Green, Rozemarijn van den Brink, Josie Talbert, and Shruti Sarode, "Regenerative agriculture: What every CCA needs to know," *Crops & Soils,* 54(4) (2021): 37–43.
5 Ken E. Giller, Renske Hijbeek, Jens A. Andersson, and James Sumberg, "Regenerative agriculture: An agronomic perspective," *Outlook on Agriculture,* 50(1) (2021): 13–25.
6 Regenerative Organic Certified, "Pilot program results," Accessed December 6, 2021. https://regenorganic.org/pilot-2/
7 "A Global Community of Leaders," B Lab, Accessed December 6, 2021. https://bcorporation.net/
8 "B Lab Directory," B Lab, Accessed December 6, 2021. https://bcorporation.net/directory
9 Julie-Anne Finan, "Certified B corps within the food industry and their innovative practices to improve environmental and social impact," (2020). https://doi.org/10.21427/26m8-2x89
10 "Coffee," Starbucks, Accessed December 7, 2021. https://www.starbucks.com/responsibility/sourcing/coffee
11 "Starbucks," Fairtrade America, Accessed December 7, 2021. https://www.fairtradeamerica.org/whyfairtrade/global-impact/impact-stories/starbucks/

Conclusion

When I was a doctoral student trying to find my way, I sat down one day in the office of my advisor, Diego Rose. His office was on one of the highest floors of the School of Public Health on Canal Street in New Orleans. From the floor to ceiling windows, you could see the twisted curves of the Mississippi River winding its way through the city to its termination in the Bayou of the gulf coast. Every time I stepped into his office, he seemed to intuit the message that I needed to hear. This time I was trying to finalize what would be the focus of my dissertation. After weighing in on a few of my propositions, he straightforwardly offered that whatever I decided to study should be something that generated intense curiosity. Something that I could dedicate many years of my life to trying to understand. Something that would propel me through the arduous path that I did not yet realize I had already gotten too far down to turn back. Perhaps most importantly, something that I believed would contribute to our understanding of sustainable food systems.

I have always been a perpetual optimist, tempered by realist tendencies. At this point, I had made it three years deep into a PhD program in Public Health Nutrition studying in the Department of Global Community Health and Behavioral Sciences. At the same time, I was also a decade deep into being involved in the social entrepreneurship community as a nonprofit co-founder and a recent transplant to the New Orleans's social impact network. Somehow, I was inhabiting both of these worlds simultaneously. One world that demands unfaltering belief that we can change the world through our work, and another that cogently questions everything and demands mountains of evidence before action. As an academic, I have ended up somewhere in between. This is what originally led me into the homesteads and farms of coffee and tea producers on opposite sides of the world. Their collective dedication to a global movement for sustainable agriculture was what propelled me through this research, and I am humbled to have had the opportunity to learn from them. Formal research is always an awkward proposition in the "real" world. You go in with your consent forms and recording devices, and you try your best to connect nonetheless to facilitate a genuine and meaningful human exchange. In both cases, I was welcomed with a sincere sense of cooperation and collaboration. I was privileged to be invited into this inspiring and yet very real world of action and innovation.

As academics, we offer lectures, presentations, and publications, with the hope that they somehow contribute to the ripple effect of change in the respective fields that we have dedicated our lives to studying. Many academics get mired in proving or disproving theories, studying barriers, offering critiques, submerged in the numbers, and railing against corrupt and defunct systems, policies, and organizations. I am still attempting to chart an alternative path, somewhere between optimism and realism that seeks to understand and share insights from the field of innovators and changemakers working at the forefront of mainstreaming the alternative.

This book has been an attempt to do just that. To share the insights gained from these two unique case studies, which highlight the collective efforts of small coffee and tea producers working with their global supply chains to support sustainability. The often-quoted Dr. Brene Brown famously mused that stories are data with a soul, and no methodology honors that more than grounded theory. She eloquently recounts that the mandate of grounded theory is to develop theories based on people's lived experiences. Here, to the best of my abilities, I have attempted to share the stories of the farmers, traders, and retailers involved in this ongoing experiment to mainstream an alternative form of agriculture and commerce. To allow their lived experience and insights to manifest a theory of change, a theory of how through collective impact, sustainability is possible to operationalize.

In closing, I am honored to be able to share the more recent words of each of the founders from these case studies. Juan Francisco Menchu Gonzalez of FECCEG and Dr. Sarath Ranaweera of Bio Foods. Each of these inspirational leaders has taken the time to reflect on their motivations, their work, and what they hope for the future. Their perspectives are more meaningful than any of the theories or frameworks that an academic could construct. In gratitude to their dedication, and to the passionate networks of farmers traders, and retailers with whom they collaborate, I conclude with their visions, shared just before the submission of this manuscript at the end of 2021.

Quetzaltenango, Guatemala, December 2, 2021

*Juan Francisco Gonzalez Menchu, CEO and
Founder of FECCEG*

During the years that I have been working with families of small coffee producers and the different situations they face each year to achieve a coffee harvest, I think that the future of small producers lies in the following actions:

1 **Community organization:** in most of the communities where we work, family production is an average of 1 ton of coffee per harvest and this makes exportation difficult both by volume and by coordination challenges, so taking advantage of the alternative markets is a means important to overcome the commercial challenges of an internationally traded product. Trust and internal organization are important to continue the work of cooperatives for the integration of families of small agricultural producers who challenge themselves to participate in the value chain for the export of their products.

2 **Care of the natural resources of the communities:** leadership must be focused on the care and conservation of the natural resources of the communities since it depends directly on them and is the local means to achieve adaptability to the adverse impacts of climate change.

3 **Promotion of organic crops and consumption in the communities:** at the same time that organic crops are promoted for export, organic crops that generate healthy food should be promoted in the communities that give the opportunity to achieve a healthier diet for families. This will improve the local economy and anticipate health by having access to better family nutrition.

4 **Promotion of quality products:** the hope for growing organic food should be reinforced by having quality crops and currently there is access to information that reinforces the collective work that promotes knowing the quality conditions that will allow them to have opportunities for stability in the export market.

5 **Compliance with certification standards:** the certification standards are continuously regulated so continuous updating and training are necessary, and compliance is a necessary condition to have the necessary approvals for the export of certified products.

6 **Inclusion of young people and women:** The inclusion of young people and women in community projects is necessary since in

rural areas the management of opportunities that promote development and development opportunities for the community with a comprehensive approach must be encouraged.

Many thanks for the opportunity that an organization such as FECCEG of Guatemala be taken into account in the systematization of a book that promotes or fosters the sustainability of rural communities, I write these lines hoping to be able to contribute in guiding the integration of projects of organizations that will work for their development through commercialization.

Colombo, Sri Lanka, November 5, 2021

Dr. Sarath Ranaweera, Chairman Bio Foods (Pvt) Ltd.

I have started the Small Organic Farmer Project with a strong concept to support organic smaller-scale producers in 1993. Then organic agriculture was defined by us as an environmentally friendly, culturally sensitive, economically viable, and socially just system with an efficient management resulting in easy traceability and transparency. When I look back on the events of the last 28 years, I have started the project with farmer leaders, direct purchase system (contract production) and farmer societies and ended up the same project by selecting the democratic society system as the best model. Marginalized Organic Producers Association (MOPA) is an independent large organic farmer organization consisting of regional and village level operating and decision-making structures. Introducing minimum farm gate prices (MFGP) to the farmers' produces was one of the key factors for the success of the project toward a sustainable model. Purchase almost all the raw materials respecting MFGP and paying higher premium prices throughout the project has resulted in building the confidence of farmers and Fairtrade premium helped a lot to develop the projects within the farming communities for the improvement of socio-economic standards of most needy producers.

Fairtrade system does not work without fairtrade supply chain. To satisfy all partners who are in the value chain as stakeholders, timely deliveries, agreed volumes, reasonable prices, and higher quality standards with consistency become essential requirements.

The MOPA was born as a marginalized small farmer project to minimize the discrepancies for the sustainability of both organizations along with Bio Foods as processor and exporter. What is the best model for small organic farmers in Sri Lanka must be decided with present changes in fair trade or any other labeling system and changing economic situation in the world.

Common FT logo used for the products from larger plantations and Small Organic Farmer Projects (SOFP) has also challenged the survival of the small farmer projects due to price pressure on processors and exporters dedicatedly work only with organic small farmer projects. Appropriate, practical, adoptable, and affordable labeling system is now essentially needed to build up trust among the stakeholders and dignity of small farmers who support biodiversity, maintain healthy soils, look after their families and surroundings.

Survival of small organic farmers has become a problem not only in the South (developing countries) but also in the North (developed countries). Understanding problems, helping each other, and uniting will be the direction for the future survival of all small organic producers.

Bibliography

Acosta-Alba, Ivonne, Joachim Boissy, Eduardo Chia, and Nadine Andrieu, "Integrating diversity of smallholder coffee cropping systems in environmental analysis," *International Journal of Life Cycle Assess*, 25 (2020): 252–266. 10.1007/s11367-01901689-5

Alkire, Sabina, Ruth Meinzen-Dick, Amber Peterman, Agnes Quisumbing, Greg Seymour, and Ana Vaz, "The women's empowerment in agriculture index," *World Development*, 52 (2013): 71–91.

Alsop, Ruth, and Nina Heinsohn, *Measuring Empowerment in Practice: Structuring Analysis and Framing Indicators*, Vol. 3510 (World Bank Publications, 2005).

B Lab, "A Global Community of Leaders," Accessed December 6, 2021: https://bcorporation.net/

Bacon, Christopher M., V. Ernesto Méndez, and Jonathan A. Fox. "Cultivating sustainable coffee: Persistent paradoxes." Confronting the Coffee Crisis: Fair Trade, Sustainable Livelihoods and Ecosystems in Mexico and Central America. MIT Press, Cambridge, MA (2008): 337–372.

Baffes, John, Bryan Lewin, and Panos Varangis, "Coffee: Market," *Global Agricultural Trade and Developing Countries*, 63, no. 13 (2004): 297.

Barr, Stewart, Andrew Gilg, and Gareth Shaw, "Citizens, consumers, and sustainability: (Re)framing environmental practice in an age of climate change," *Global Climate Change*, 21 (2011): 4.

Basiago, Andrew D., "Economic, social, and environmental sustainability in development theory and urban planning practice," *Environmentalist,* 19, no. 2 (1998): 145–161.

Behera, Kambaska Kumar, Afroz Alam, Sharad Vats, Hunuman Pd Sharma, and Vinay Sharma, "Organic farming history and techniques," In *Agroecology and Strategies for Climate Change* (pp. 287–328), Springer, Dordrecht, 2012.

Besky, Sarah, *Tasting Qualities: The Past and Future of Tea* (University of California Press, 2020).

Bilfield, Alissa, David Seal, and Diego Rose, "From agency to empowerment: Women farmers' experiences of a fairtrade coffee cooperative in

Guatemala," *Journal of Gender, Agriculture, and Food Security*, 5, no. 1 (2020): 1–13. doi: 10.19268/JGAFS.512020.1

Boaventura, Patricia Silva Monteiro, Carla Caires Abdalla, Cecilia Lobo Araujo, and Jose Sarkis Arakelian, "Value co creation in the specialty coffee value chain: the third-wave coffee movement," *Revista de Administração de Empresas* 58 (2018): 254–266.

Boyer, Robert, Nicole Peterson, Poonam Arora, and Kevin Caldwell, "Five approaches to social sustainability and an integrated way forward," *Sustainability*, 8 (2016):1–18.

Browne, Angela W., Phil J.C. Harris, Anna H. Hofny-Collins, Nick Pasiecznik, and Ron R. Wallace, "Organic production and ethical trade: Definition, practice and links," *Food Policy*, 25, no. 1 (2000): 69–89.

Brundtland, G., "Report of the world commission on environment and development: Our common future," United Nations General Assembly document A/42/427 (1987).

Bunn, Christian, Mark Lundy, Peter Läderach, Pablo Fernández Kolb, Fabio Castro-Llanos, and Dylan Rigsby. "Climate Smart Coffee in Guatemala." (2019). Accessible online: https://cgspace.cgiar.org/handle/10568/103771

Buttel, Frederick H., and Kenneth A. Gould, "Global social movement(s) at the crossroads: Some observations on the trajectory of the anti-corporate globalization movement," *Journal of World-Systems Research*, 10, no. 1 (2004): 37–66. doi:10.5195/jwsr.2004.309

Chamarbagwala, Rubiana, and Hilcias Moran, "The human capital consequences of civil war: Evidence from Guatemala," *Journal of Development Economics*, 94, no. 1 (2011): 41–61. 10.1016/j.jdeveco.2010.01.005

Cherrington-Hollis, Seren. *A Dark History of Tea* (Pen and Sword History, 2022).

Comparable Indicators," *Oxford Development Studies*, 35, no. 4 (2007): 379–403.

Crosier, Alan, Hiroshi Ashihara, and Francisco Tomas-Barberan, *Teas, Cocoa and Coffee: Plant Secondary Metabolites and Health* (Wiley, 2011).

Curtin, Phillip. *The Rise and Fall of the Plantation Complex: Essays in Atlantic History* (Cambridge: Cambridge University Press, 1998). doi: 10.1017/CBO9780511811914

De Chiara, Alessandra, "Collective impact approach: A 'tool' for managing complex problems and business clusters sustainability," *Metropolitan Universities*, 28, no. 4 (2017): 101–114.

Deb, Saptashish, and K.R. Jolvis, "Review of withering in the processing of black tea," *Journal of Biosystems Engineering*, 41, no. 4 (2016): 365–372. doi: 10.5307/JBE.2016.41.4.365

Demeter USA, "Demeter Farm and Processing Standard," (2021) Accessed online: https://www.demeterusa.org/learn-more/biodynamic-farm-standard.asp

Dragusanu, Raluca, Daniele Giovannucci, and Nathan Nunn, "The economics of fair trade," *Journal of Economic Perspectives*, 28, no. 3 (2014): 217–236.

Drew, Liam, "The growth of tea," *Nature*, 566, no. 7742, Accessed September 15, 2021: *Gale Academic OneFile*, link.gale.com/apps/doc/A573274317/AONE?u=anon~8ac87c45&sid=googleScholar&xid=febd75 7

Dulekha, Kasturiratne, "An overview of the Sri Lankan tea industry: An exploratory case study," *The Marketing Review*, 8, no. 4 (2008): 367–381.

Elson, R.E., and Ary Kraal, *The Politics of Colonial Exploitation: Java, the Dutch, and the Cultivation System* (SEAP Publications Cornell University, 1992).

European Union, "Aims of the EU Organic Logo," (2021) Accessed online: https://ec.europa.eu/info/food-farmingfisheries/farming/organic-farming/organic-logoen

Fairtrade America, "Starbucks," Accessed December 7, 2021: https://www.fairtradeamerica.org/whyfairtrade/global-impact/impact-stories/starbucks/

Fairtrade International, "Coffee,"(2018) Accessed online: https://www.fairtrade.net/product/coffee

Fairtrade International, "Fair trade Standards for Small-scale Producer Organizations," (2019) Accessed online: https://www.fairtrade.net/fileadmin/user_upload/content/2009/standards/SPO_EN.pdf

Fairtrade International, "Fair trade Trader Standards," Accessed online: Fair trade International. "Fair trade Standards for Small-scale Producer Organizations". Accessed online (2019)

Feenberg, Anne-Marie, "'Max Havelaar: An anti-imperialist novel," *MLN*, 112, no. 5 (1997): 817–835. http://www.jstor.org/stable/3251421

Finan, Julie-Anne, "Certified B corps within the food industry and their innovative practices to improve environmental and social impact" (2020).

Fischer, Edward, "Quality and inequality: Creating value worlds with third wave coffee," *Socio-Economic Review*, 19, no. 1 (2021): 111–131.

Fischer, Edward F. "Guatemalan political economies and the world system," In: *Cultural Logics and Global Economies: Maya Identity Thought and Practice*, 65–82 (New York, USA: University of Texas Press, 2021) 10.7560/725300-005.

Fischer, Edward F., and Bart Victor, "High-end coffee and small holding growers in Guatemala," *Latin American Research Review*, 49, no. 1 (2014): 155–177. http://www.jstor.org/stable/43670157

Food and Agriculture Organization, *Agricultural Cooperatives: Paving the Way for Food Security and Rural Development* (Rome, Italy, 2012).

Food and Agriculture Organization. "Food-Based Dietary Guidelines: Dietary Guidelines and Sustainability,"(2021) Accessed online: https://www.fao.org/nutrition/education/food-dietaryguidelines/background/sustainable-dietary-guidelines/en/

Gereffi, Gary, and Joonkoo Lee, "Economic and social upgrading in global value chains and industrial clusters: Why governance matters," *Journal of Business Ethics*, 133, no. 1 (2016): 25–38.

Gerlicz, Andrew, "Diversification Strategies and Contributions of Coffee Income to Poverty Alleviation Among Smallholders in Northern Huehuetenango and Quiche Departments, Guatemala," (2016).

Giller, Ken E., Renske Hijbeek, Jens A. Andersson, and James Sumberg, "Regenerative agriculture: An agronomic perspective," *Outlook on Agriculture*, 50, no. 1 (2021): 13–25.

Gomiero, Tiziano, Maurizio G. Paoletti, and David Pimentel, "Energy and environmental issues in organic and conventional agriculture," *Critical Reviews in Plant Sciences*, 27, no. 4 (2008): 239–254.

Green, Thomas, Rozemarijn van den Brink, Josie Talbert, and Shruti Sarode, "Regenerative agriculture: What every CCA needs to know," *Crops & Soils*, 54, no. 4 (2021): 37–43.

Halberg, Niels, "Assessment of the environmental sustainability of organic farming: Definitions, indicators and the major challenges," *Canadian Journal of Plant Science*, 92, no. 6 (2012): 981–996.

Harper, Gemma C., and Aikaterini Makatouni, "Consumer perception of organic food production and farm animal welfare," *British Food Journal* (2002): 287–299.

Heckman, Joseph, "A history of organic farming: Transitions from Sir Albert Howard's war in the soil to USDA National Organic Program," *Renewable Agriculture and Food Systems*, 21, no. 3 (2006): 143–150.

Herath, Deepananda, and Alfons Weersink, "From plantations to smallholder production: The role of policy in the reorganization of the Sri Lankan tea sector," *World Development*, 37, no. 11 (2009): 1759–1772.

Hindsley, Paul, David McEvoy, and Ashton Morgan, "Consumer demand for ethical products and the role of cultural worldviews: The case of direct-trade coffee," *Ecological Economics* (Elsevier), 17 (2020): 1–10.

Holland, Emil, Chris Kjeldsen, and Søren Kerndrup, "Coordinating quality practices in direct trade coffee," *Journal of Cultural Economy*, 9, no. 2 (2016): 186–196. https://www.fairtrade.net/fileadmin/user_upload/content/2009/standards/SPO_EN.pdf

Hutchins, Margot J., and John W. Sutherland, "An exploration of measures of social sustainability and their application to supply chain decisions," *Journal of Cleaner Production*, 16, no. 15 (2008): 1688–1698.

Hutter, Hans-Peter, Abdul Wali Khan, Kathrin Lemmerer, Peter Wallner, Michael Kundi, and Hanns Moshammer, "Cytotoxic and genotoxic effects of pesticide exposure in male coffee farmworkers of the Jarabacoa Region, Dominican Republic," *International Journal of Environmental Research and Public Health*, 15, no. 8 (2018): 1641.

Ibrahim, Solava, and Sabina Alkire, "Agency and empowerment: A proposal for internationally comparable indicators," *Oxford Development Studies*, 35, no. 4 (2007): 379–403.

Iles, A., and M. Montenegro de Wit, "Sovereignty at what scale? An Inquiry into International Federation of Organic Agriculture Movement," *Principles of Organic Agriculture* (2005) Accessed online: http://www.ifoam.org/about_ifoam/principles/.

Iles, A., and Montenegro de Wit, M. (2015) Sovereignty at What Scale? An Inquiry into Multiple Dimensions of Food Sovereignty. *Globalizations*, 12:4, 481–497, DOI: 10.1080/14747731.2014.957587.

Interview Participant. 2017. Anonymous coffee farmer, Cooperative Association in Huehuetenango, Guatemala, in discussion with the author. March. Transcript available upon request.

Interview Participant 1. 2017. Tea federation founder, Kandy, Sri Lanka, in discussion with the author. November. Transcript available upon request.

Interview Participant 1. 2018. Anonymous tea farmer, Cooperative Association in Kandy, Sri Lanka, in discussion with the author. December. Transcript available upon request.

Interview Participant 10. 2017. Anonymous coffee farmer, Cooperative Association in Huehuetenango, Guatemala, in discussion with the author. March. Transcript available upon request.

Interview Participant 10. 2018. Anonymous tea farmer, Cooperative Association in Kandy, Sri Lanka, in discussion with the author. December. Transcript available upon request.

Interview Participant 10. 2019. Anonymous tea retailer, Video Interview, in discussion with the author. July. Transcript available upon request

Interview Participant 11. 2018. Anonymous tea farmer, Cooperative Association in Kandy, Sri Lanka, in discussion with the author. December. Transcript available upon request.

Interview Participant 12. 2017. Anonymous coffee farmer, Cooperative Association in Huehuetenango, Guatemala, in discussion with the author. March. Transcript available upon request.

Interview Participant 12. 2017. Anonymous coffee federation manager, Quetzaltenango, Guatemala, in discussion with the author. March. Transcript available upon request.

Interview Participant 13. 2017. Anonymous coffee retailer, Video Interview, in discussion with the author. June. Transcript available upon request.

Interview Participant 14. 2017. Anonymous coffee farmer, Cooperative Association in Huehuetenango, Guatemala, in discussion with the author. March. Transcript available upon request.

Interview Participant 14. 2017. Anonymous coffee retailer, Video Interview, in discussion with the author. June. Transcript available upon request.

Interview Participant 14. 2018. Anonymous tea farmer, Cooperative Association in Kandy, Sri Lanka, in discussion with the author. December. Transcript available upon request.

Interview Participant 16. 2017. Anonymous coffee farmer, Cooperative Association in Huehuetenango, Guatemala, in discussion with the author. March. Transcript available upon request.

Interview Participant 16. 2018. Anonymous tea farmer, Cooperative Association in Kandy, Sri Lanka, in discussion with the author. December. Transcript available upon request.

Interview Participant 17. 2017. Anonymous coffee farmer, Cooperative Association in Huehuetenango, Guatemala, in discussion with the author. March. Transcript available upon request.

Interview Participant 18. 2017. Anonymous coffee exporter, Antigua, Guatemala, in discussion with the author. April. Transcript available upon request.

Interview Participant 2. 2017. Anonymous coffee farmer, Cooperative Association in Huehuetenango, Guatemala, in discussion with the author. March. Transcript available upon request.

Interview Participant 2. 2017. Anonymous tea federation staff, Kandy, Sri Lanka, in discussion with the author. November. Transcript available upon request.

Interview Participant 2. 2018. Anonymous tea farmer, Cooperative Association in Kandy, Sri Lanka, in discussion with the author. December. Transcript available upon request.

Interview Participant 2. 2018. Anonymous tea federation manager, Kandy, Sri Lanka, in discussion with the author. December. Transcript available upon request.

Interview Participant 20. 2017. Anonymous coffee farmer, Cooperative Association in Huehuetenango, Guatemala, in discussion with the author. March. Transcript available upon request.

Interview Participant 22. 2017. Anonymous coffee farmer, Cooperative Association in Huehuetenango, Guatemala, in discussion with the author. March. Transcript available upon request.

Interview Participant 22. 2018. Anonymous tea buyer, Video Interview, in discussion with the author. December. Transcript available upon request.

Interview Participant 23. 2017. Anonymous coffee farmer, Cooperative Association in Huehuetenango, Guatemala, in discussion with the author. March. Transcript available upon request.

Interview Participant 23. 2018. Anonymous tea farmer, Cooperative Association in Kandy, Sri Lanka, in discussion with the author. December. Transcript available upon request.

Interview Participant 3. 2017. Anonymous coffee farmer, Cooperative Association in Huehuetenango, Guatemala, in discussion with the author. March. Transcript available upon request.

Interview Participant 3. 2018. Anonymous tea farmer, Cooperative Association in Kandy, Sri Lanka, in discussion with the author. December. Transcript available upon request.

Interview Participant 3. 2019. Anonymous tea retailer, Video Interview, in discussion with the author. July. Transcript available upon request.

Interview Participant 4. 2018. Anonymous tea farmer, Cooperative Association in Kandy, Sri Lanka, in discussion with the author. December. Transcript available upon request.

Interview Participant 5. 2019. Anonymous tea retailer, Video Interview, in discussion with the author. July. Transcript available upon request.

Interview Participant 7. 2018. Anonymous tea farmer, Cooperative Association in Kandy, Sri Lanka, in discussion with the author. December. Transcript available upon request.

Interview Participant 7. 2019. Anonymous tea retailer, Video Interview, in discussion with the author. July. Transcript available upon request

Interview Participant 8. 2017. Anonymous coffee farmer, Cooperative Association in Huehuetenango, Guatemala, in discussion with the author. March. Transcript available upon request.

Interview Participant 8. 2017. Anonymous coffee retailer, Video Interview, in discussion with the author. June. Transcript available upon request.

Interview Participant 8. 2018. Anonymous tea farmer, Cooperative Association in Kandy, Sri Lanka, in discussion with the author. December. Transcript available upon request.

Interview Participant 9. 2017. Anonymous coffee farmer, Cooperative Association in Huehuetenango, Guatemala, in discussion with the author. March. Transcript available upon request.

Interview Participant 9. 2017. Anonymous coffee roaster, Video Interview, in discussion with the author. June. Transcript available upon request.

Jaffee, Daniel, *Brewing Justice* (University of California Press, 2014).

Jaffee, Daniel. *Brewing Justice: Fair Trade Coffee, Sustainability and Survival* (UC Press, 2016).

Japanese Agricultural Standards. "Japanese Organic Standard for Plant Production,"(2017) Accessed online: https://aco.net.au/Documents/JAS/JAS_Standard_producer_1605_revised_2017.pdf

Jegathesan, Mythri, *Tea and Solidarity: Tamil Women and Work in Postwar Sri Lanka* (University of Washington Press, 2019).

Joachim, Sauerborn, "Review of history and recent development of organic farming worldwide," *Agricultural sciences in China*, 5, no. 3 (2006): 169–178.

Johnston, Josee, "Consuming Global Justice: Fair Trade shopping and alternative development." In: *Protest and Globalization: Prospects for Transnational Solidarity* (Sydney: Pluto Press Australia, 2002).

Kanapathipillai, Valli, *Citizenship and Statelessness in Sri Lanka: The Case of the Tamil Estate Workers* (Anthem Press, 2009).

Kania, J., and M. Kramer, "Collective impact". *Stanford Social Innovation Review*, Winter (2004) Accessed online: http://ssir.org/articles/entry/collective_impact

Kituyi, Mukhisa. "Fifty years of promoting trade and development." *In International Trade Forum*, no. 2, p. 30. International Trade Centre, 2014.

Koeler, Jeff, *Where the Wild Coffee Grows* (Bloomsbury, USA, 2017).

Kullak, Franziska S., Julia A. Fehrer, Jonathan J. Baker, Herbert Woratschek, and Joana Sam-Cobbah, "Shaping market systems for social change in emerging economies," *Industrial Marketing Management*, 100 (2022): 19–35.

Lamine, Claire, "Transition pathways towards a robust ecologization of agriculture and the need for system redesign. Cases from organic farming and IPM," *Journal of Rural Studies*, 27, no. 2 (2011): 209–219.

Latruffe, Laure, Ambre Diazabakana, Christian Bockstaller, Yann Desjeux, John Finn, Edel Kelly, Mary Ryan, and Sandra Uthes, "Measurement of sustainability in agriculture: A review of indicators," *Studies in Agricultural Economics*, 118, no. 3 (2016): 123–130.

Leu, Andre, "Regenerative agriculture movements," *Organic Food Systems* (2020): 21. https://foodsecurity.ac.za/wp-content/uploads/2019/11/Organic-Food-Systems-Meeting-the-Needs-of-Southern-Africa.Auerbach.10.2019.pdf#page=56

Lotter, Donald W., "Organic agriculture," *Journal of Sustainable Agriculture*, 21, no. 4 (2003): 59–128.

Low, Will, and Davenport, Eileen, "Mainstreaming fair trade: Adoption, assimilation, appropriation," *Journal of Strategic Marketing*, 14 (2007): 315–327.

Luttikholt, L. W. M., *Principles of Organic Agriculture as Formulated by the International Federation of Organic Agriculture Movements* (International Federation of Organic Agriculture Movements (IFOAM), 2007).

Lyon, Sarah, Josefina Aranda Bezaury, and Tad Mutersbaugh, "Gender Equity in Fair trade organic Coffee Producer Organizations: Cases from Mesoamerica," *Geoforum*, 41, no. 1 (2010): 93–103. doi: 10.1016/j.geoforum.2009.04.006

Lyon, Sarah, *Coffee and Community: Maya Farmers and Fair Trade Markets* (Boulder: University Press of Colorado, 2011).

Malhotra, Anju, Sidney Ruth Schuler, and Carol Boender, "Measuring women's empowerment as a variable in international development," In *Background Paper Prepared for the World Bank Workshop on Poverty and Gender: New Perspectives*, 28 (2002).

Martin, Laura. *The History of Tea: The Life and Times of the World's Favorite Beverage* (Tuttle Press, 2018).

McCreery, David, "State Power, Indigenous Communities, and Land in Nineteenth Century Guatemala, 1820-1920," In:*Guatemalan Indians and the State: 1540-1988*, edited by Carol A. Smith, 96–115 (New York, USA: University of Texas Press, 2021). 10.7560/727441-009.

Meegahakumbura, Muditha K., Moses C. Wambulwa, Miao-Miao Li, Kishore K. Thapa, Yong-Shuai Sun, Michael Möller, Jian-Chu Xu, Jun-Bo Yang, Jie Liu, Ben-Ying Liu, De-Zhu Li, and Lian-Ming Gao, "Domestication origin and breeding history of the tea plant (*Camellia sinensis*) in China and India based on nuclear microsatellites and cpDNA Sequence data," *Frontiers in Plant Science*, 8, no. 2270 (2018). 10.3389/fpls.2017.02270

Monier-Dilhan, Sylvette, and Fabian Bergès, "Consumers' motivations driving organic demand: Between self interest and sustainability," *Agricultural and Resource Economics Review*, 45, no. 3 (2016): 522–538.

Mori, Koichiro, and Aris Christodoulou, "Review of sustainability indices and indicators: Towards a new city sustainability index," *Environmental Impact Assessment Review*, 32 (2012):94-1-6.

Morris, Jonathan, "We Consumers—Tastes, Rituals, and Waves," In *The Craft and Science of Coffee*, edited by Britta Folmer, 457–491 (Academic Press, 2017).

National Research Council, *Toward Sustainability: A Plan for Collaborative Research on Agriculture and Natural Resource Management* (National Academies Press, 1991).

Naylor, Lindsay, "Some are more fair than others": Fair trade certification, development, and northsouth subjects, *Agriculture and Human Values*, 31, no. 2 (2013): 273–284. doi: 10.1007/s10460013-9476-0

Nussbaum, Martha, "Women and equality: The capabilities approach." *International Labour Review*, 138 (1999): 227.

Pendergrast, Mark, *Uncommon Grounds: The History of Coffee and How it Transformed Our World* (Basic Books, 2010).

Petchers, Seth, and Shayna Harris, "The roots of the coffee crisis," *Confronting the Coffee Crisis: Fair Trade, Sustainable Livelihoods and Ecosystems in Mexico and Central America* (MIT Press, Cambridge, MA, 2008).

Photovoice Focus Group Participant 1. 2017. Anonymous coffee farmer, Cooperative Association in Huehuetenango, Guatemala, in discussion with the author. April. Transcript available upon request.

Photovoice Focus Group Participant 4. 2017. Anonymous coffee farmer, Cooperative Association in Huehuetenango, Guatemala, in discussion with the author. April. Transcript available upon request.

Photovoice Focus Group Participant 5. 2017. Anonymous coffee farmer, Cooperative Association in Huehuetenango, Guatemala, in discussion with the author. April. Transcript available upon request.

Pimentel, David, Laura Westra, and Reed F. Noss, eds. *Ecological Integrity: Integrating Environment, Conservation, and Health* (Island Press, 2000).

Place, Frank, Meinzen-Dick, Ruth Suseela, and Ghebru, Hosaena, 2021. "Natural resource management and resource rights for agriculture," IFPRI book chapters, in: Agricultural development: New perspectives in a changing world, chapter 18, pages 595–628, International Food Policy Research Institute (IFPRI).

Ponnamperuma, Sumedha, Sonal Katyal, and Mangla Snajay Kumar, "Economic and social evolution of Sri Lanka from colonial rule to a liberalized economy," *PaKsoM* (2020). ISBN 978-86-80616-06-3 159

Purvis, Ben, Yong Mao, and Darren Robinson, "Three pillars of sustainability: In search of conceptual origins," *Sustainability Sciences*, 14 (2019): 681–695. 10.1007/s11625-018-0627-5

Rapone, Anita, and Charles R. Simpson, "Women's response to violence in Guatemala: Resistance and rebuilding," *International Journal of Politics,*

Culture, and Society, 10, no. 1 (1996): 115–140. http://www.jstor.org/stable/20019876

Rappaport, Erika, *A Thirst for Empire: How Tea Shaped the Modern World* (Princeton University Press, 2017). 10.1515/9781400884858

Raynolds, Laura T., "Consumer/producer links in fair trade coffee networks," *Sociologia Ruralis*, 42, no. 4 (2002): 404–424. doi:10.1111/1467-9523.00224

Redfern, Andy, and Paul Snedker, *Creating Market Opportunities for Small Enterprises: Experiences of the Fair Trade Movement* (ILO, Geneva, 2002).

Regenerative Organic Certified, "*Pilot Program Results*," Accessed December 6, 2021: https://regenorganic.org/pilot-2/

Reji, Edakkandi Meethal, "Value Chains and Small Enterprise Development: Theory and Praxis" *American Journal of Industrial and Business Management*, 3, no. 1, (2013): 28–35. doi: 10.4236/ajibm.2013.31004.

Reynolds, Laura, "The Globalization of Organic Agro-Food Networks," *World Development*, 32, no. 5 (2004): 725–743. 10.1016/j.worlddev.2003.11.008

Roden, C., *Coffee* (Penguin Books, London, 1981).

Ronchi, Loraine, *The Impact of Fair Trade on Producers and their Organizations: A Case Study with Coocafe in Costa Rica* (Policy Research Unit, University of Sussex, UK, 2002).

Rose, Sarah, *For All the Tea in China* (Penguin Books, 2010).

Roseberry, William, "The rise of yuppie coffees and the reimagination of class in the United States," *American Anthropologist*, 98, no. 4 (1996): 762–775. http://www.jstor.org/stable/681884.

Sabiha, Noor-E., Ruhul Salim, Sanzidur Rahman, and Maria Fay Rola-Rubzen, "Measuring environmental sustainability in agriculture: A composite environmental impact index approach," *Journal of Environmental Management*, 166 (2016): 84–93.

Schifferstein, H., Alie Boer, and M. Lemke "Conveying information through food packaging: A literature review comparing legislation with consumer perception," *Journal of Functional Foods*, 86 (2021): 10.1016/j.jff.2021.104734

Scoones, I., (1998). "Sustainable Rural Livelihoods: A Framework for Analysis," IDS Working Paper 72, Brighton: IDS. Accessed online: https://opendocs.ids.ac.uk/opendocs/handle/20.500.12413/3390

Sen, Amartya, (1999). "Commodities and Capabilities," *OUP Catalogue, Oxford University Press, number 9780195650389.*

Sen, Amartya, "Well-being, agency and freedom: The Dewey lectures," *The Journal of Philosophy*, 82, no. 4 (1985): 169–221.

Sen, Debarati, *Everyday Sustainability: Gender Justice and Fairtrade Tea in Darjeeling* (SUNY Press, 2017).

Shafie, Farah Ayuni, and Denise Rennie, "Consumer perceptions towards organic food," *Procedia-Social and Behavioral Sciences*, 49 (2012): 360–367.

Shiferaw, Bekele A., Julius Okello, and Ratna V. Reddy. "Adoption and adaptation of natural resource management innovations in smallholder agriculture: reflections on key lessons and best practices." *Environment, Development and Sustainability* 11, no. 3 (2009): 601–619.

Shreck, Aimee, "Resistance, redistribution, and power in the fair trade banana initiative," *Agriculture and Human Values*, 22, no. 1 (2005): 17–29. doi:10.1 007/s10460 004-7227-y

Sigley, Gary, "Tea and China's rise: Tea, nationalism and culture in the 21st century," *International Communication of Chinese Culture*, 2 (2018): 319–341. Accessed online: 10.1007/s406360150037-7

Soulé, Emma, Philippe Michonneau, Nadia Michel, and Christian Bockstaller, "Environmental sustainability assessment in agricultural systems: A conceptual and methodological review." *Journal of Cleaner Production* 325 (2021): 129291. doi: https://doi.org/10.1016/j.jclepro.2021.129291

Specialty Coffee Association, *Facts and Figures 2018*(2021). Accessed online: https://sca.coffee/research/specialtycoffee-facts-figures

Specialty Coffee Association, *Coffee Flavor Wheel* (1995). Accessed online: http://www.scaa.org/?d=scaa-flavorwheel&page=resources

Starbucks, "Coffee," Accessed December 7, 2021: https://www.starbucks.com/responsibility/sourcing/coffee

Steinberg, Michael, Taylor, Matthew, and Moran-Taylor, Michelle, "Coffee and Mayan cultural commodification in Guatemala," *Geographical Review*, 104, no. 3 (2014): 361–373. doi: 10.1111/j.19310846.2014.12031.x

Stirling, Andrew, "The appraisal of sustainability: Some problems and possible response," *Local Environment*, 4 (1999): 111–135.

Tencati, Antonio, and Laszlo Zsolnai, "The collaborative enterprise," *Journal of Business Ethics*, 85, no. 3 (2009): 367–376.

Ukers, William, *All About Coffee* (The Tea and Coffee Trade Journal Company, New York, 1922).

Ukers, William, *All About Tea* (The Tea & Coffee Trade Journal Co., New York, 1935).

UNDSD, "Indicators of sustainable development: Guidelines and methodologies," Accessed December 7, 2021: https://sdgs.un.org/

United Nations Department of Economic and Social Affairs, "Social Development for sustainable development," Accessed December 7, 2021: https://www.un.org/development/desa/dspd/2030agenda-sdgs.html

United States Department of Agriculture, "What the USDA organic label means,"(2021) Accessed online:https://www.usda.gov/media/blog/2012/03/22/organic-101-what-usda-organic-label-means

Uspenski, Maria, "Specialty Tea – The Yin to Coffee's Yang in the Third Wave," *The Tea Spot* (2019) Accessed online: https://www.theteaspot.com/blogs/steep-it-loose/specialty-tea-the-yin-to-coffee-s-yang-in-the3rd-wave

Van Cauwenbergh, Nora K. Biala, Charles Bielders, V. Brouckaert, L. Franchois, V. Garcia Cidad, Martin Hermy, et al., "SAFE—A hierarchical framework for assessing the sustainability of agricultural systems," *Agriculture, Ecosystems & Environment*, 120, no. 2–4 (2007): 229–242.

Vega, Fernando, "The rise of coffee." *American Scientist*, 96, no. 2 (2008): 138–145.

Wild, Anthony, *Coffee, a Dark History* (WW Norton, 2004).

Willer, H., J. Travnicek, C. Meier, and B. Schlater, *The World of Organic Agriculture: Statistics and Emerging Trends for 2021*. Accessed online November 2021: https://www.fibl.org/fileadmin/documents/shop/1150organic-world-2021.pdf

Willson, Ken C., and Michael N. Clifford, eds., *Tea: Cultivation to Consumption* (Springer Science & Business Media, 2012).

Winslow, Deborah, and Woost, Michael, *Economy, Culture, and Civil War in Sri Lanka* (Indiana University Press, 2004).

World Fair Trade Organization, "Annual Report 2017," (2017) Accessed online: https://wfto.com/sites/default/files/WFTO%20Annual%20Report%202017.pdf

World Fair Trade Organization, "Definition of Fair Trade,"(2019) Accessed online: https://wfto.com/fairtrade/definition-fair-trade

Yadav, Shailesh Kumar, Arnab Banerjee, Manoj Kumar Jhariya, Abhishek Raj, Nahid Khan, Ram Swaroop Meena, and Sandeep Kumar, "Agroecology towards environmental sustainability," In *Sustainable Intensification for Agroecosystem Services and Management*, pp. 323–352 (Springer, Singapore, 2021).

Index

For Product Safety Concerns and Information please contact our EU
representative GPSR@taylorandfrancis.com
Taylor & Francis Verlag GmbH, Kaufingerstraße 24, 80331 München, Germany